LA BONNE CUISINE

Soups

100 CLASSIC AND ORIGINAL RECIPES

whitecap

contents

chilled
soups

fresh vegetables

Some people wince at the word "vegetable." Yet, our dishes would be very drab and dull if we deprived them of the incredible diversity of flavors, colors and shapes that exist in the form of vegetables. Some vegetables are particularly nutritious, and a pleasure to cook.

nutritional benefits

Cabbage: a source of vitamins, mineral salts, and fiber; its sulfur compounds exert a detoxifying action.

Zucchini: hydrates and restores moisture, thanks to its high water and potassium content. It provides magnesium, calcium, and fiber.

Spinach: rich in water, it also provides fiber, linolenic acid, vitamins, mineral salts, and trace elements. It is not recommended to reheat cooked spinach (nitrites).

Fennel: full of nutritional benefits such as fiber and polyunsaturated fatty acids. It stimulates digestion, reduces inflammation of the stomach, and has diuretic properties.

Fava beans: rich in carbohydrates, protein, and dietary fiber. They are a source of vitamins and contain a number of mineral salts, beginning with iron.

Black radishes: rich in carbohydrates and magnesium. They provide mineral salts, trace elements, and sulfur compounds. Since they are eaten raw, all their health benefits are preserved.

choosing and using

Whatever the fresh vegetable, the first rule is to use seasonal produce. Fresh food is much tastier when it's at the peak of maturity, and seasonal food is more reasonable. Choose local producers with few intermediaries because the products will be very fresh and, consequently, of better nutritional quality.

Organic produce guarantees that the vegetables were grown without the use of pesticides and chemical fertilizers. They must still be washed beforehand, but avoid soaking them for too long, overcooking them, preparing them in advance, or reheating. Slow cooking methods, like steaming or stewing, help preserve their nutritional qualities.

Vary the ways in which you slice vegetables (round slices, spaghetti-like strips, cubes, sticks) and prepare them raw or cooked, in salads or soups, as a side-dish, puréed, wrapped in tinfoil, in gratins, soufflés, savory pies, sauces, with pasta or cereal, seasoned with garlic, onion, spices and herbs . . . there are endless possibilities.

chilled asparagus soup

EASY AND AFFORDABLE - PREPARATION: 15 MIN - COOKING TIME: 25 MIN
CHILLING TIME: 2 H

SERVES 4

600 g (1½ lb) green asparagus • half a bunch of radishes, with tops • 1 dessert spoon (2 tsp) olive oil • 1 dessert spoon (2 tsp) crème fraîche (heavy sour cream) with 15% fat content • 4 dessert spoons (2¾ Tbsp) radish sprouts (or alfalfa sprouts, found in the fresh food section of supermarkets with the herbs and lettuce) • salt • freshly ground pepper

Cut the radishes into very thin, round slices and set aside. Rinse and drain the green tops. In a stewpot, heat 1.2 L (5 cups) of salted water. Cook the peeled and rinsed asparagus with the green radish tops for 7 minutes.

Drain the asparagus and remove tips (which should measure about 3 cm / 1¼ iches each). Return the stalks to the stewpot and leave to cook for another 15 minutes over a low heat. Mix the soup, add the cream, season with salt and pepper, and place in the refrigerator for 2 hours.

Sauté the asparagus tips in the oil for 2 to 3 minutes. Pour the chilled soup into individual bowls and garnish with the asparagus tips, the sliced radish, and a dessert spoonful of radish or alfalfa sprouts.

SUGGESTED WINE PAIRING: a white meursault

chilled almond soup

EASY AND ECONOMICAL - PREPARATION: 15 MIN - CHILLING TIME: 1 H

SERVES 4

250 g (½ lb) blanched almonds • 150 g (5 oz) bread • 2 garlic cloves • 15 cl (⅔ cup) olive oil • 1 dessert spoon (2 tsp) sherry vinegar • 1 bunch of green grapes • salt

Soak the bread in water. Peel the garlic cloves and place them, with the almonds and bread (drained), in a food processor. Season with salt. Avoid heating the food in the processor by mixing for a short time, then stopping and mixing again, etc. As soon as the mixture is smooth, continue mixing and drizzle with the olive oil and the sherry vinegar. Add 1 L (4 cups) of very cold water and place the soup in the refrigerator for at least 1 hour.

Meanwhile, peel and seed the grapes. Just before serving, place some grapes on top of the chilled soup.

SUGGESTED WINE PAIRING: a fino sherry

CVF RECOMMENDATION: check the seasoning before adding the grapes, it may be necessary to add a little vinegar and salt.

chilled green soup

EASY AND ECONOMICAL - PREPARATION: 15 MIN - CHILLING TIME : 1 H

SERVES 6
6 green apples • 1 cucumber • 2 tomatoes • 4 white onions • 2 limes, divided •
2 dessert spoons (1¼ Tbsp) olive oil • 12 sprigs cilantro, divided • 3 drops
Tabasco sauce • salt • freshly ground pepper

Slice off the top of each apple and carefully remove the flesh with a small spoon, leaving a
thin layer inside so as not to damage the skin. Remove the core and the seeds. Squeeze
1 lime and brush the inside of the apple with the lime juice.

In a food processor, mix the apple flesh with the onions, peeled cucumber (set aside
12 slices for later), 6 sprigs of cilantro, oil, juice of the second lime, Tabasco sauce, salt,
and pepper until the mixture is smooth. Place in the refrigerator for 1 hour.

Immerse the tomatoes in boiling water for 30 seconds before peeling and quartering.
Remove the seeds, dice, and place in the refrigerator.

Serve the soup in the empty apples and decorate with the diced tomato, sliced cucumber,
and the rest of the cilantro. Serve chilled.

SUGGESTED WINE PAIRING: a dry jurançon

chilled pistou soup

EASY AND ECONOMICAL - PREPARATION: 30 MIN - COOKING TIME: 25 MIN
CHILLING TIME: 2 H

SERVES 6

200 g (7 oz) slender French green beans • 300 g (10 oz) yellow French beans •
200 g (7 oz) runner beans • 3 potatoes • 1 zucchini • 4 tomatoes • 2 onions •
1 bunch mixed herbs • 3 garlic cloves • ½ dessert spoon (1 tsp) olive oil •
1 dessert spoon (2 tsp) pistou sauce • 1 bunch basil • 50 g (1¾ oz) shaved
parmesan • salt • freshly ground pepper

String the beans and slice into sections. Add to 1.5 L (6 cups) of salted, boiling water with
the mixed herbs and peeled and diced potatoes. Cook for 10 minutes. Add the washed
and diced zucchini. Cook for another 5 minutes then drain the vegetables and strain the
bouillon. Set aside separately.

Immerse the tomatoes in boiling water for 30 seconds before peeling. Remove the seeds
and dice. Heat the oil in a stewpot and sauté the chopped onions over a low heat. Add the
peeled, crushed garlic cloves and the diced tomato. Leave to simmer for 5 minutes then
add the vegetable bouillon and bring to a boil.

Turn off the heat. Add the pistou, season with salt and pepper, and leave to cool. Return
the vegetables to the bouillon and place in the refrigerator for 2 hours. Divide the soup
equally into individual bowls. Sprinkle with the basil and parmesan and serve.

SUGGESTED WINE PAIRING: a côtes de provence rosé

CVF RECOMMENDATION: pistou sauce comes in a glass jar and is generally found in
supermarkets with other sauces and condiments. Pistou sauce is a mixture of basil, garlic,
olive oil, and parmesan. It is somewhat similar to Genoese "pesto," except that the latter
contains pine nuts as well.

white Andalusian gazpacho

EASY AND ECONOMICAL - PREPARATION: 20 MIN - COOKING TIME: 3 MIN
CHILLING TIME: 1H30

SERVES 4

1 cucumber · 150 g (5 oz) bread · 100 g (3½ oz) blanched almonds · 30 g
(1 oz) pine nuts · 30 g (1 oz) raisins · 5 dessert spoons (¼ cup) olive oil ·
2 garlic cloves · 2 dessert spoons (1¼ Tbsp) sherry vinegar · 100 g (3½ oz)
green grapes · salt · freshly ground pepper

In a frying pan, dry roast the pine nuts for a few minutes and allow to cool on a paper
towel. Mix them with the raisins and coarsely chop. Set aside.

Discard the bread crust and soak the bread in water. Peel and cut the cucumber into large
cubes. Set aside.

Seed the grapes. Drain the bread and mix it in a food processor with the almonds, grapes,
peeled garlic cloves, oil, and vinegar. Season with salt and pepper. Add 75 cl (3¼ cups) of
ice cold water and mix again until the soup becomes thick, smooth, and creamy. Place the
gazpacho in the refrigerator for 1½ hours.

Before serving, divide the pine nut and raisin mixture equally into 4 bowls. Pour the chilled
gazpacho over the top, sprinkle with the diced cucumber, and serve immediately.

SUGGESTED WINE PAIRING: a white irouléguy

CVF RECOMMENDATION: slice some French bread and rub with garlic. Fry in a little olive
oil and serve with the gazpacho.

refreshing cucumber and pine nut soup

EASY AND ECONOMICAL - PREPARATION: 10 MIN - COOKING TIME: 3 MIN

SERVES 4

2 large cucumbers • 50 g (1¾ oz) pine nuts • 50 g (1¾ oz) raisins • 1 bunch
basil • 3 dessert spoons (2 Tbsp) olive oil • 2 chicken bouillon cubes • salt •
freshly ground pepper • a few drops of Tabasco sauce (preferably green) •
2 slices farmhouse bread

Dilute the bouillon cubes in 20 cl (¾ cup) of very hot water. Leave to cool. Peel the
cucumbers, slice in half, remove the seeds, and dice. In a food processor, mix the
cucumber with the bouillon and Tabasco sauce. Season with a little salt and pepper. Add
the basil leaves (reserve a few for garnish), oil, and half of the raisins, and mix again. Place
the soup in the refrigerator.

Dry roast the pine nuts in a frying pan over a low heat and leave to cool on a paper towel.
Pour the chilled cucumber soup into a serving bowl or individual bowls. Sprinkle with
the raisins and roasted pine nuts and garnish with some basil leaves. Serve with slices of
toasted farmhouse bread.

SUGGESTED WINE PAIRING: a sylvaner

CVF RECOMMENDATION: green Tabasco sauce, which only appeared on the market in
recent years, is made from the jalapeño pepper. It is very fragrant and less spicy than the
red chili pepper. Both the red and green varieties are natural products from Louisiana.
The peppers are crushed, salted, and placed in oak barrels where they are left to age for
3 years. The mixture is then strained and mixed with a little vinegar. No food coloring,
preservatives or fat is added to these spicy sauces, which are very popular in the United
States.

chilled avocado soup

EASY AND ECONOMICAL - PREPARATION: 20 MIN - COOKING TIME: 5 MIN

SERVES 6

4 ripe avocados • 2 chicken bouillon cubes • 1 lemon • 6 sprigs cilantro, divided • 20 cl (¾ cup) table cream • 1 pinch Espelette pepper • 3 slices farmhouse bread • 2 slices Parma ham • 2 dessert spoons (1¼ Tbsp) olive oil • salt

Dilute the bouillon cubes in 70 cl (3 cups) of hot water and leave to cool. Rinse the lemon, grate half of its zest and juice. Halve the avocados, remove the pit and scoop out the flesh. Remove the leaves from the cilantro.

Place the avocado, lemon zest and juice, half of the cilantro, the cooled bouillon, and the cream in a mixing bowl (or blender). Season with salt and blend until the mixture is smooth and creamy. Transfer to individual serving bowls and place in the refrigerator.

Just before serving, take the thinly sliced ham and sauté in a frying pan with 1 dessert spoon (2 tsp) of oil. Remove the crust from the bread and fry in the same pan with the rest of the oil. Lay the strips of ham on the bread and place on top of the soup. Sprinkle with a little Espelette pepper, garnish with the rest of the cilantro, and serve immediately.

SUGGESTED WINE PAIRING: a white mâcon

tomatoes

The tomato is often considered a vegetable; however, from a botanical point of view, it is, in fact, a fruit. It is a species of herbaceous plant belonging to the Solanaceae nightshade family and originating in the north west of South America. There are several varieties, the main ones being **Solanum lycopersicum esculentum**, large tomatoes, and **Solanum lycopersicum cerasiforme**, the cherry tomato. In France, tomatoes can be found all year round. Those sold from March to November are mostly of French origin, whereas those sold between December and February are imported, mainly from Morocco and Spain.

nutritional benefits

Tomatoes are full of nutritional benefits. They are made up of 95 percent water and have a calorie intake of only 18 calories per 100 g (3½ oz).

Tomatoes contain high levels of minerals and vitamins A, C, and E. They are also very rich in potassium, which facilitates muscle contraction, including the heart, and helps improve the transmission of nerve impulses.

Tomatoes contain a high level of copper, which acts as a catalyst in the synthesis of hemoglobin and in collagen formation.

choosing and using

The best tomatoes are those that have ripened in the sun and are available between July and September. Choose local producers rather than large retailers because they sometimes offer original, less common varieties.

Rinse tomatoes under cold, running water, then cut into thin slices, drizzle with a little olive oil, and sprinkle with a few basil leaves.

Essential elements of many slow-cooked or simmered dishes, like bolognese or espagnole sauce, tomatoes are the perfect ingredient to go with your pasta dishes.

Cut them into quarters, drizzle with olive oil, sprinkle with herbs and a few cloves of garlic, then bake in the oven for 2 hours at 150°C (300°F).

Stuffed tomatoes are one of the emblematic dishes of the South of France – fill with a mixture of meat, onions, and herbs, then bake in the oven at 150°C (300°F) for about 35 minutes.

In chilled soups, like the traditional Spanish gazpacho, the perfect blend of tomato with cucumber, spicy sauce, and herbs results in a delicious, flavorful dish. In hot, tomato-based soups, bring out the flavor by adding chervil or other aromatic herbs.

gazpacho with tomato sorbet

EASY AND ECONOMICAL · PREPARATION: 20 MIN · CHILLING TIME: 3 H

SERVES 6

1.5 kg (3 lb) tomatoes · 1 large cucumber · 1 red pepper · 1 green pepper · 1 celery stalk · 2 fresh onions · 2 garlic cloves · 125 g (¼ lb) white breadcrumbs · juice of 1 lemon, divided · 4 dessert spoons (2¾ Tbsp) extra-virgin olive oil · ½ dessert spoon (1 tsp) sherry vinegar · salt · freshly ground pepper

Immerse the tomatoes in boiling water for 30 seconds before peeling and removing the seeds. Purée the tomato with a mixer. Add a few drops of lemon juice and stir. Pour a third of the mixture into an ice cube tray and place in the freezer. Pour the rest of the tomato purée into a large bowl.

Wash the other vegetables and cut the celery into pieces. Halve the peppers, remove the seeds and the white pith, and slice into strips. Peel and quarter the onions. Peel the cucumber and cut it into slices 2 cm (¾ inch) thick. Peel the garlic cloves. Set aside a few strips of pepper and some cucumber slices for garnish.

Transfer all the vegetables to a food processor and purée until smooth. Sprinkle the breadcrumbs into the large bowl with the tomato purée. Add the puréed vegetables, the rest of the lemon juice, salt, and vinegar, and mix.

Place the bowl in the refrigerator for at least 3 hours. Serve the soup in individual bowls, drizzle with a little oil, add 1 or 2 tomato ice cubes, and season with pepper just before serving.

SUGGESTED WINE PAIRING: a côteaux du languedoc rosé

tomato gazpacho with garlic mayonnaise

EASY AND ECONOMICAL · PREPARATION: 20 MIN · CHILLING TIME: 12 H

SERVES 6

1 kg (2¼ lb) small ripe tomatoes · 4 small fresh onions · 1 small cucumber ·
2 green peppers · 2 slices stale farmhouse bread, torn into pieces · 1 garlic
clove · 4 dessert spoons (2¾ Tbsp) sherry vinegar · 20 cl (¾ cup) olive oil

For the garlic mayonnaise: 4 garlic cloves · 1 egg yolk · 20 cl (¾ cup) olive oil ·
salt · freshly ground pepper

Peel the cucumber, cut it in half to remove the seeds, and dice the flesh. Peel and chop
the onions. Wash and dry the peppers, cut them into cubes, and remove the seeds and
white pith. Wash, dry, and quarter the tomatoes. Peel the garlic and crush with the flat side
of a broad knife.

Place the vegetables in a bowl and add the vinegar, oil, and the small pieces of bread.
Season with salt and pepper, mix, cover with plastic wrap, and leave to stand in the
refrigerator for 12 hours.

When the time is up, prepare the garlic mayonnaise: peel the garlic cloves and crush with
a mortar and pestle. Add the salt, pepper, and egg yolk, and slowly pour in the oil while
continuously stirring.

Using either an electric or hand blender, mix the vegetable gazpacho with 1 L (4 cups)
of very cold water. Add the garlic mayonnaise and blend again, or serve it on the side so
guests can dollop it on top. Serve chilled.

SUGGESTED WINE PAIRING: a corbières rosé

gazpacho style soup

EASY AND ECONOMICAL · PREPARATION: 20 MIN · CHILLING TIME: 4H

SERVES 4

800 g (1¾ lb) very ripe tomatoes · 1 red pepper · 1 green pepper · 1 cucumber ·
4 fresh onions · 1 celery stalk · 2 cloves new garlic · juice of ½ lemon · 1 dessert
spoon (2 tsp) sun-dried tomato dip (sold in a glass jar at the delicatessen or
in the gourmet food section) · 6 sprigs basil · ½ dessert spoon (1 tsp) sherry
vinegar · 10 cl (½ cup) olive oil · salt · freshly ground pepper

Wash the tomatoes and remove the stems. Cut them into quarters and remove the seeds.
Wash the peppers, remove the seeds and white pith; slice into strips, then into small pieces.
Peel the cucumber and slice. Cut the celery into slices. Peel the garlic and onions.

Place all the vegetables in the bowl of a food processor or, preferably, a blender. Add the sun-
dried tomato dip, lemon juice, vinegar, oil, basil leaves, and season with salt and pepper.

Blend at a high speed until you obtain the desired consistency (reasonably smooth,
depending on your taste). Place in the refrigerator for at least 4 hours before serving.

SUGGESTED WINE PAIRING: a costières de nîmes rosé

green tomato tartare, yellow tomato soup and red tomato ice cubes

EASY AND ECONOMICAL - PREPARATION: 30 MIN - CHILLING TIME: 2 H
COOKING TIME: 5 MIN

SERVES 4

150 g (5 oz) green tomatoes (green zebra variety, if possible) • 400 g (14 oz) yellow tomatoes (pineapple variety, if possible) • 150 g (5 oz) red tomatoes • 50 g (1¾ oz) sun-dried tomatoes • juice of 1 lemon, divided • 2 sprigs thyme, divided • 1 garlic clove • 1 dessert spoon (2 tsp) olive oil • a few drops of Tabasco sauce • salt • freshly ground pepper

Wash and dry the tomatoes. After removing the stalks, cut them separately: dice the green tomatoes and cut the red and yellow ones into small pieces. Peel the garlic. Two hours in advance, place the red tomatoes, the sun-dried tomatoes, and a few drops of Tabasco sauce in a blender. Season with salt and pepper and blend until the coulis is smooth. Pour into an ice cube tray and place in the freezer for 2 hours.

Prepare the soup: place the yellow tomatoes in a saucepan with 15 cl (⅔ cup) of water, the garlic, and 1 sprig of thyme. Add salt and bring to a boil. Turn off the heat, remove the garlic and thyme and pour into the blender. Add half the lemon juice and blend until the soup is smooth. Season with pepper and keep warm in the saucepan over a low heat.

Prepare the tartare: chop the leaves of the second sprig of thyme. Season the green tomatoes with salt, pepper, olive oil, thyme, and the remaining lemon juice. Mix and set aside at room temperature.

To serve, shape the tartare into domes in the center of 4 soup bowls, top with a red tomato ice cube and pour the yellow soup around the dome.

SUGGESTED WINE PAIRING: a white viognier

Alberto's gazpacho

EASY AND ECONOMICAL - PREPARATION: 10 MIN - CHILLING TIME: 12H

SERVES 6

1.2 kg (2½ lb) ripe tomatoes • 4 eggs • 2 garlic cloves • 120 g (4¼ oz) bread •
20 cl (¾ cup) fruity olive oil, divided • 6 dessert spoons sherry vinegar •
3 sprigs fresh thyme, divided • salt • freshly ground pepper

Boil the eggs for 10 minutes in boiling, salted water. Place them under cold running water, remove the shells and quarter. Slice the bread, toast, and leave to cool. Remove the leaves from the sprigs of thyme.

Remove the stalk from the tomatoes by slightly slitting the skin with a sharp knife. Immerse them for a few seconds in a saucepan of boiling water, drain and peel. Cut into small pieces and remove some of the seeds. Peel and finely chop the garlic.

Place the tomatoes, eggs, garlic, bread, vinegar, half the thyme, and half the oil in a bowl with a pinch of salt. Cover and place in the refrigerator for 12 hours.

When the time is up, add the remaining oil and pepper to the bowl and mix the ingredients with a hand or electric blender. Sprinkle the gazpacho with the rest of the thyme leaves and serve chilled.

SUGGESTED WINE PAIRING: a white côtes de gascogne

seafood
soups

crustaceans

Crustaceans are arthropods. Their bodies are rigid, except for certain, flexible areas, which allow them to move various parts of their body. There are more than 50,000 species, most of which are marine species.

nutritional benefits

Crab: like most seafood, crab provides a significant amount of protein and has a low fat content. It is also an excellent source of vitamin B12, selenium, and other nutrients.

Prawns: rich in vitamins and minerals, including niacin, vitamin B12, phosphorus, and selenium, they are also an excellent source of protein. Furthermore, their low fat content makes them ideal for a healthy diet.

Mussels: notably rich in vitamin B12, selenium, manganese, and several other vitamins and minerals, they are particularly nutritious.

Scallops: rich in essential minerals, which are necessary for a healthy diet, they contain a high level of protein and a low level of fat.

Lobster: highly nutritious, they are an excellent source of several vitamins and minerals such as copper, selenium, zinc, and vitamin B12.

choosing and using

Most of these crustaceans or shellfish can be simply steamed or cooked in a court-bouillon (briefly boiled liquid) and served with a homemade mayonnaise.

This delicious seafood also goes very well with exotic food products, citrus fruits, and spices.

Prawns, scallops, or crab can be marinated raw in a mixture of lime, ginger, and olive oil, then simply cooked in a frying pan or on a hot griddle.

Keep the shells of your lobsters, prawns, or crab and use them to prepare tasty soups and bisques. Served with toasted bread and a spicy Provençal "rouille" sauce made from olive oil, breadcrumbs, garlic, saffron, and chili peppers, they make delicious starters.

creamy vegetable and mussel soup

EASY AND ECONOMICAL - PREPARATION: 10 MIN - COOKING TIME: 30 MIN

SERVES 4

1 kg (2¼ lb) mussels • 300 g (10 oz) zucchini • 200 g (7 oz) celery stalks •
250 g (½ lb) leeks • 150 g (5 oz) potatoes • 40 cl (1¾ cups) coconut milk •
10 sprigs of cilantro • 2 garlic cloves • 2 dessert spoons (1¼ Tbsp) olive oil • salt

Discard the ends of the zucchini, clean the leeks and celery stalks, and peel the potatoes.
Cut the vegetables into 0.5 cm (¼ inch) cubes and rinse. Peel the garlic and slice into thin,
short strips. Remove the leaves from the cilantro and set aside.

Heat the oil in a casserole dish, add the vegetables, stir, and cook for 5 minutes. Add
½ L (5¼ quarts) of water, season with salt, stir, and cook for 20 minutes.

Scrub the mussels and wash several times. Place them in a stewpot over a high heat until
they open, then remove from the heat. Strain the mussel juice over the vegetables in the
casserole dish and stir. Remove the shells of a third of the mussels and leave the others
whole for garnish.

Pour the coconut milk over the vegetables, add the cilantro and, when boiling, add the
mussels; stir and remove from the heat. Serve hot.

SUGGESTED WINE PAIRING: a condrieu

pumpkin and mussel soup

EASY AND ECONOMICAL - PREPARATION: 15 MIN - COOKING TIME: 30 MIN

SERVES 4

500 g (1 lb) pumpkin flesh • 2 L (8 cups) bouchot mussels • 1 chicken bouillon cube • ½ lemon • small bunch of chives • salt • freshly ground pepper

Dilute the bouillon cube in 25 cl (1 cup) water. Peel the pumpkin, cut the flesh into cubes, and place in a casserole dish with the bouillon. Bring to a boil, reduce heat, and cook for about 25 minutes until the pumpkin is very tender and starts to fall apart.

Meanwhile, scrub the mussels, remove beards, wash thoroughly, and place in a stewpot. Heat over a low heat for 10 to 15 minutes until they open. Remove them from the pot with a skimming ladle; set aside a few for garnish and remove the shells from the rest. Strain the juice to remove all traces of sand.

Remove the pumpkin from the casserole dish. Place it with the shelled mussels and 2 dessert spoons (1¼ Tbsp) of lemon juice in the bowl of a food processor and mix thoroughly until the soup thickens.

Warm the soup for a few minutes over a low heat in the casserole dish. Season with salt and serve in 4 warm bowls. Garnish with chives and mussels, season with pepper, and serve.

SUGGESTED WINE PAIRING: a white sancerre

CVF RECOMMENDATION: you can use this recipe to prepare a clam soup.

curried mussel soup

EASY AND ECONOMICAL - PREPARATION: 20 MIN - COOKING TIME: 20 MIN

SERVES 4

2 L (8 cups) bouchot mussels • 40 cl (1¾ cups) dry white wine • 15 cl (⅔ cup) heavy sour cream, divided • 2 egg yolks • 4 small white onions • 2 dessert spoons (1¼ Tbsp) fish bouillon powder • 25 g (⅞ oz) butter • 1 level dessert spoon (2 tsp) curry powder • 1 bay leaf • salt • freshly ground pepper

Peel the small white onions and slice in two. Scrub the mussels, debeard, and wash. Place them in a stewpot with the white wine, bay leaf and onions. Cover the pot and place over a high heat. Stir occasionally, until all the mussels have opened up.

Drain the mussels and onions by straining their cooking juice. Pour the juice into a saucepan over a high heat, add 50 cl (2 cups) water and the fish bouillon. Bring to a boil and simmer for 10 minutes, stirring regularly.

In another saucepan, melt the butter and add the curry. Remove from the heat and, while whisking, add two-thirds of the sour cream. Pour this mixture into the saucepan of bouillon while stirring, and allow to boil for 1 minute. Reduce the heat and leave to simmer.

Whisk the egg yolks with the remaining cream and a ladle of bouillon. Transfer to the stewpot and add the mussels and onions. Season with salt and pepper and heat (do not boil) for 2 minutes. Check the seasoning and serve in a tureen.

SUGGESTED WINE PAIRING: a white jura wine

chilled cream of shrimp soup

EASY AND REASONABLE - PREPARATION: 30 MIN - COOKING TIME: 25 MIN

SERVES 6

400 g (14 oz) shrimp (rather large) • 120 g (4¼ oz) shelled peas (fresh or frozen) • 8 green asparagus spears • 150 g (5 oz) button mushrooms • 4 small white onions • 50 g (1¾ oz) butter • 50 cl (2 cups) light cream • 1 dessert spoon (2 tsp) tomato purée • 1 bunch of chervil • salt • freshly ground pepper

Remove the heads from the shrimp and set aside. Peel the tails. Peel and thinly slice the onions, clean the mushrooms and slice into strips. Peel the asparagus and only keep the first third of the stalk below the tip. Place in the refrigerator.

Sauté the onions, mushrooms, and shrimp heads for 5 minutes in the butter. Add the tomato purée and the cream. Leave to simmer for 12 minutes, then mix and strain into a bowl. Cool down the mixture by placing the bowl in a container of ice cold water.

Immerse the asparagus and peas in a large stewpot of boiling salted water and cook for about 12 minutes. Drain and carefully cool down with ice cold water.

Check the seasoning of the shrimp cream, divide it into bowls, garnish with the asparagus, peas, and chervil, and serve.

SUGGESTED WINE PAIRING: a pinot gris

scallop soup for the fall

EASY AND REASONABLE - PREPARATION: 20 MIN - COOKING TIME: 25 MIN

SERVES 4

1 pumpkin slice (1.2 kg / 2½ lb) • 2 carrots • 24 scallops • 2 garlic cloves •
½ dessert spoon (1 tsp) ground cumin • 1 bunch of mixed herbs • 10 cl
(½ cup) liquid sour cream • 1 dessert spoon (2 tsp) olive oil • salt • freshly
ground pepper

Peel the pumpkin and cut the flesh into cubes. Scrape, wash, and cut the carrots into
round slices. Peel the garlic cloves. Place the pumpkin cubes, slices of carrot, and the
garlic in a stewpot with the bouquet garni. Season with salt, pepper, and cumin. Add
1.5 L (6 cups) of water and simmer for 20 minutes.

Once cooked, mix the soup, add the sour cream, and set aside. Remove the scallops from
the shells, rinse, and gently pat dry with a paper towel. Heat the oil in a frying pan and
sauté the scallops for a few seconds over a high heat. Season with salt and pepper.

Before serving, warm the soup for a few minutes over a low heat. Pour into individual soup
bowls, garnish with the scallops, and serve immediately.

SUGGESTED WINE PAIRING: a limoux

chicken broth with mussels and vermicelli

EASY AND ECONOMICAL · PREPARATION: 30 MIN · COOKING TIME: 2 H 05

SERVES 6

1.5 kg (3 lb) chicken wings (or 1 chicken) · 1.2 kg (2½ lb) mussels · 200 g
(7 oz) vermicelli · 2 onions · 1 garlic bulb · 4 celery stalks · 2 shallots · 1 small
bunch of chives · 6 sprigs of chervil · 1 bunch of mixed herbs (chives, chervil,
thyme, rosemary, bay leaf) · peppercorns · salt · freshly ground pepper

Bring 3 L (12 cups) of water to a boil. Add the chicken wings (or trussed chicken), onions,
shallots, garlic head (entirely peeled), celery, bunch of mixed herbs, and ½ teaspoon of
peppercorns. Cover and slow cook for 2 hours to prevent the broth from becoming cloudy.

Clean the mussels, debeard, and heat in a frying pan for 3 minutes so they open up. Set
aside a few mussels in their shells for garnish and remove the shells of the rest. Strain the
juice. Divide the mussels into bowls with a little chicken broth. Strain the cooked broth,
bring to a boil, and season with salt and pepper. Add the vermicelli (120 g / 4¼ oz per liter
of broth) and cook for 2 minutes. Serve the vermicelli on top of the mussels and sprinkle
with mixed herbs. Garnish with the whole mussels and serve immediately.

SUGGESTED WINE PAIRING: a white mâcon

cream of oyster soup

QUITE EASY AND REASONABLE - PREPARATION: 30 MIN - COOKING TIME: 45 MIN

SERVES 4

24 cupped oysters (n° 2) • 2 sole carcasses (ask your fishmonger) • 5 egg yolks • 1 bunch of chervil • ½ onion • 20 cl (¾ cup) vermouth • 20 cl (¾ cup) table cream • 3 dessert spoons (2 Tbsp) olive oil • salt • freshly ground pepper

Peel and slice the onion. Remove the leaves from the chervil. Tie up the stems and place them in a casserole dish with the oil, onion, rinsed carcasses, and vermouth. Reduce by half. Add 80 cl (3½ cups) of water and 2 pinches of salt and pepper. Bring to a simmer, skim, and cook for 25 minutes. Strain the bouillon and set aside 60 cl (2½ cups). Add water, if necessary.

Shuck the oysters and discard the shells. Drain the oysters through a fine mesh sieve over a stewpot to recover their juice. Bring the juice to a simmer and poach the oysters for 1 minute. Drain and set aside.

Heat the bouillon in a saucepan. In a bowl, whisk the egg yolks with the cream and add 2 ladles of bouillon. Transfer to the saucepan. Whisk over a low heat for 5 minutes until the mixture thickens. Remove from the heat and add the oyster juice. Divide the oysters into bowls, add the soup, garnish with chervil leaves, and serve.

SUGGESTED WINE PAIRING: a muscadet sèvre et maine

mussel soup

EASY AND ECONOMICAL - PREPARATION: 30 MIN - COOKING TIME: 20 MIN

SERVES 4

1.5 kg (3 lb) bouchot mussels • 2 onions • 1 celery stalk • 50 cl (2 cups) dry white wine • 20 g (¾ oz) butter • 25 cl (1 cup) table cream • 1 pinch of saffron pistils • 1 small bunch of flat-leaf parsley • salt • freshly ground pepper

Clean and rinse the mussels several times, debeard, then drain. Rinse and dry the parsley, remove the leaves, and chop. Peel and chop the onions. Remove the strings from the celery and thinly slice.

Melt the butter in a casserole dish. Sauté the onions and celery until soft, add half the chopped parsley and the saffron. Add the white wine, bring to a boil, then add the mussels. Stir, then cover and leave the mussels to open over a high heat (about 10 minutes), shaking occasionally to evenly distribute the heat. When all the mussels have opened, turn off the heat.

Discard the mussel shells. Strain the cooking juices through a muslin cloth to remove any traces of sand. Using an electric or hand blender, mix the mussel meat with the cooking juices. Transfer the mixture to the casserole dish, add the cream, 25 cl (1 cup) of boiling water, salt, and pepper. Stir and leave to simmer over a low heat until the soup is smooth and creamy. Sprinkle with the remaining chopped parsley and serve piping hot.

SUGGESTED WINE PAIRING: a muscadet sèvre et maine sur lie (Loire Valley white wine)

spicy seafood soup

EASY AND ECONOMICAL - PREPARATION: 20 MIN - COOKING TIME: 20 MIN

SERVES 4

1.5 kg (3 lb) bouchot mussels • 2 onions • 1 celery stalk • 50 cl (2 cups) dry
white wine • 30 g (1 oz) butter • 25 cl (1 cup) table cream •1 dessert spoon
(2 tsp) fish bouillon powder • ½ dessert spoon (1 tsp) ground Espelette
pepper • 2 pinches of saffron • 4 slices of toasted bread • 50 g (1¾ oz)
parmesan • salt • freshly ground pepper

Scrub the mussels under cold water, debeard, and rinse thoroughly several times. Peel the
onions, remove the strings from the celery, and finely chop both.

Melt the butter in a casserole dish and brown the onions and celery. Sprinkle with the
saffron, add the wine, salt, and pepper (five twists of the pepper mill), and bring to a boil.
Add the mussels and cook over a high heat, stirring occasionally, until they have all opened
up. Discard the shells and set the mussels aside.

Strain the cooking juices and add to the casserole dish with 25 cl (1 cup) of water, the fish
bouillon, cream, and Espelette pepper, and simmer for 5 minutes without covering. Add the
mussels and heat for 2 minutes.

Slice the parmesan with a vegetable peeler. Divide the soup into 4 soup bowls and serve
with the toasted bread, topped with the parmesan shavings.

SUGGESTED WINE PAIRING: a white irouléguy

bourride sétoise
(traditional fish soup from Sète)

A LITTLE EXPENSIVE BUT EASY • PREPARATION: 20 MIN • COOKING TIME: 20 MIN

SERVES 6

2 kg white fish (monkfish, whiting, tilapia) • 1 large onion • 1 tomato • 2 garlic cloves • 1 bunch of mixed herbs (thyme, bay leaf, parsley) • 1 sprig of fennel • 1 orange peel • 6 egg yolks • 6 slices of bread • olive oil • salt • freshly ground pepper

For the garlic mayonnaise: 6 garlic cloves • 1 egg yolk • olive oil • salt

Prepare the garlic mayonnaise: using a mortar and pestle, crush the 6 garlic cloves and add a pinch of salt. Beat the garlic purée and 1 egg yolk with olive oil until you obtain a mayonnaise. Set aside.

Ask the fishmonger to scale and gut the fish. Wash and cut the fish into large pieces. Place them in a saucepan with 2 tablespoons of olive oil, the mixed herbs, onion, garlic, peeled and seeded tomato, fennel, and 5 cm (2 inches) of orange peel. Cover well with hot water. Season with salt and pepper and cook in rapidly boiling water for about 15 minutes. Remove the fish from the saucepan and keep warm. Strain the cooking juices. Place the slices of bread in a tureen.

In a large saucepan, take a wooden spoon and mix the equivalent of about 2 dessert spoons (1¼ Tbsp) per person of garlic mayonnaise with the egg yolks. Gradually add the fish bouillon. Stir over a very low heat, without boiling, until the mixture thickens and coats the wooden spoon. Pour the soup into the tureen and add the fish. Serve with the rest of the garlic mayonnaise in a separate bowl.

SUGGESTED WINE PAIRING: a white bandol

clam and orange soup

EASY AND REASONABLE - PREPARATION: 10 MIN - SOAKING TIME: 30 MIN
COOKING TIME: 30 MIN

SERVES 6

500 g (1 lb) clams • 1 orange • 1 celery stalk • 1 onion • 1 garlic clove • 4 small
potatoes • 2 sachets shellfish bouillon (Ariake) • 25 cl (1 cup) table cream •
20 g (¾ oz) butter • 2 dessert spoons (1¼ Tbsp) olive oil • 1 sprig of fresh
thyme • 1 pinch of saffron pistils • salt • freshly ground pepper

Soak the clams in salted cold water for 30 minutes, stirring regularly. Drain and cook in a
saucepan with 1 glass of water until they have opened. Strain the cooking juices. Dilute
the shellfish bouillon in 80 cl (3½ cups) of boiling water, add the cooking juices from the
clams, and set aside.

Wash the orange and wipe dry. Grate half the zest and squeeze the fruit. Remove the
strings from the celery and peel the onion, garlic, and potatoes. Dice the potatoes and chop
the celery, onion, and garlic. Sauté the chopped vegetables with the zest in a casserole
dish with the butter and oil. Add the potatoes, bouillon, saffron, salt, and pepper. Cover and
cook for 20 minutes.

Remove the shells from the clams. Place them in the casserole dish with the orange juice
and the cream and continue cooking for 3 minutes over a very low heat. Sprinkle with the
fresh thyme and serve.

SUGGESTED WINE PAIRING: a bandol rosé

cream of scallop, carrot and cumin soup

EASY AND ECONOMICAL · PREPARATION: 15 MIN · COOKING TIME: 25 MIN

SERVES 6

6 large carrots · 18 scallops with shells · 3 dessert spoons (2 Tbsp) heavy cream · 2 vegetable bouillon cubes · 30 g (1 oz) butter · 1 dessert spoon (2 tsp) olive oil · ½ dessert spoon (1 tsp) ground cumin · ½ dessert spoon (1 tsp) cumin seeds · salt · sea salt (fleur de sel) · freshly ground pepper

Ask your fishmonger to shuck the scallops. Rinse, pat dry, and place in the refrigerator. Peel the carrots and cut into round slices.

Heat the oil in a stewpot and sauté the carrots for several minutes while stirring. Add 1.5 L (6 cups) of hot water and the bouillon cubes. Cook over a low heat for 20 to 25 minutes.

Mix the ingredients of the stewpot, add the cream, ground cumin, salt, and pepper, and cook over a low heat.

Heat the butter in a frying pan and sear each side of the scallops for 30 seconds.

Divide the scallops equally into 6 soup bowls. Add the hot carrot cream and sprinkle with the cumin seeds and sea salt. Serve.

SUGGESTED WINE PAIRING: a white reuilly

cream of clam, bacon, chervil and dill soup

EASY AND REASONABLE - PREPARATION: 40 MIN - RESTING TIME: 30 MIN
COOKING TIME: 20 MIN

SERVES 4

1 kg (2¼ lb) clams • 4 sprigs of dill • 1 bunch of chervil, divided • 2 small
zucchini • 1 large ordinary potato • 2 slices of bacon • 1 garlic clove • 1 small
onion • 20 g (¾ oz) butter • 1 dessert spoon (2 tsp) olive oil • 10 cl (½ cup)
light cream • Espelette pepper • coarse sea salt

Place the clams in a basin of cold water with 3 tablespoons of coarse salt and leave them
to soak for 30 minutes, stirring occasionally. Drain and place them in a saucepan with
15 cl (⅔ cup) of water over a high heat.

Cover and cook for about 4 minutes, until they have all opened up. Strain the cooking
juices and set aside. Remove the shells. Coarsely chop the chervil and dill leaves. Wash,
dry, and dice the zucchini. Peel and dice the potato.

Peel and chop the garlic and onion and sauté over a low heat in a frying pan with the
butter and oil. Add the chervil (set aside a little), dill, diced potatoes, and zucchini. Add the
cooking juices from the clams, about 60 cl (2½ cups) of water, and 2 pinches of pepper.
Cover and cook for 15 minutes.

Remove from the heat, add the cream, and mix (with a hand mixer). Warm the soup over a
low heat. Fry the bacon in a frying pan until crispy, then let it cool.

Coarsely crumble the bacon with your fingers. Pour the soup into individual bowls
and sprinkle with the bacon. Add the clams, garnish with the rest of the chervil, and serve
immediately.

SUGGESTED WINE PAIRING: a muscadet sèvre et maine

surimi and ginger soup

EASY AND ECONOMICAL - PREPARATION: 10 MIN - COOKING TIME: 10 MIN

SERVES 4

300 g (10 oz) shredded surimi • 150 g (5 oz) potatoes • 40 cl (1¾ cups)
water • 1 heaped teaspoon ground ginger • salt • freshly ground pepper

Peel the potatoes and cut them into small cubes. Place in a saucepan with 40 cl (1¾
cups) of water, the salt, and ginger. Cook for about 10 minutes. Add the shredded surimi
and pepper.

Mix all the ingredients with a hand blender. Serve piping hot with croutons.

SUGGESTED WINE PAIRING: a white sylvaner

radish and salmon roe gazpacho

EASY AND ECONOMICAL - PREPARATION: 30 MIN - COOKING TIME: 20 MIN
CHILLING TIME: 1 H

SERVES 4

1 bunch of red radishes • 350 g (12¼ oz) black radishes (2 medium-sized) •
50 g (1¾ oz) salmon roe • 25 cl (1 cup) light cream • 25 cl (1 cup) whole milk •
coarse sea salt • white pepper

Trim and wash the red radishes. Set aside 8 and dice the rest. Cut a large slice of black
radish with its skin and set aside. Peel the rest and dice.

Pour the milk and cream into a saucepan. Add the diced radish and leave to simmer for
20 minutes. Season with 1 level teaspoon of coarse sea salt and some pepper.

Cut the 8 red radishes and the round slice of black radish into short, thin strips. Blend the
milk, cream, and radish sauce. Leave to cool and place in the refrigerator for at least 1 hour.

To serve, divide the chilled radish gazpacho into small glasses or bowls, and garnish with
the julienne radish strips and salmon roe.

SUGGESTED WINE PAIRING: a muscadet sèvre et maine

cream of porcini mushroom and salmon soup

EASY AND REASONABLE · SOAKING TIME: 30 MIN · PREPARATION: 20 MIN
COOKING TIME: 30 MIN

SERVES 6

60 g (2 oz) dried porcini mushrooms · 100 g (3½ oz) smoked salmon · 1 small shallot · 3 chicken bouillon cubes · 3 dessert spoons (2 Tbsp) olive oil, divided · 30 g (1 oz) butter · 15 cl (⅔ cup) light cream · salt · freshly ground pepper

Soak the porcini mushrooms for 30 minutes in warm water, then drain. Peel and chop the shallot. In a large saucepan, heat the butter and 2 dessert spoons (1¼ Tbsp) of oil. Sauté the shallot and the chopped mushrooms until their water content has evaporated. Set aside.

Dilute the bouillon cubes in 1 L (4 cups) of boiling water. Pour the bouillon over the mushrooms, season with salt and pepper, and cook for 15 minutes.

Cut the salmon into thin strips. Heat the remaining oil in a nonstick frying pan and cook the salmon for 2 minutes on each side.

Mix the mushrooms with the bouillon until smooth, add the cream and heat for 3 to 4 minutes. Pour into soup bowls, garnish with the salmon strips and serve piping hot.

SUGGESTED WINE PAIRING: a white châteauneuf du pape

leek and crab soup with chantilly cream and herbs

EASY AND AFFORDABLE - PREPARATION: 20 MIN - COOKING TIME: 35 MIN

SERVES 6

500 g (1 lb) leeks • 250 g (½ lb) potatoes (BF15 or charlotte) • 200 g (7 oz) crab meat (canned or frozen) • 80 g (2¾ oz) butter • 4 sprigs of dill • salt • freshly ground pepper

For the chantilly cream: 25 cl (1 cup) very cold light cream • 2 dessert spoons (1¼ Tbsp) finely chopped herbs (parsley, chives)

Clean, wash and cut the leeks into ½ cm (¼ inch) slices. Peel, wash, and cut the potatoes into ½ cm (¼ inch) cubes. Heat 1.5 L (6 cups) of water in a saucepan.

Melt the butter in a stewpot, add the leeks, and stir until soft. Add 10 cl (½ cup) of hot water, cover and cook for 10 minutes. Add the diced potatoes, season with salt and pepper, stir, and pour in the remaining hot water. Cook for another 20 minutes.

Meanwhile, flake the crab meat with a fork. Just before the leeks have finished cooking, whip the cream until firm, season with salt, and add the chopped herbs.

Divide the leeks, potatoes, and bouillon into 6 soup bowls, add the crab, place a dessert spoon (2 tsp) of whipped cream in the center, garnish with the chopped dill, and serve.

SUGGESTED WINE PAIRING: a crémant du jura

refreshing smoked trout soup

EASY AND REASONABLE - PREPARATION: 15 MIN - COOKING TIME: 5 MIN
CHILLING TIME: 2 H

SERVES 4

200 g (7 oz) smoked trout · 1 portion black radish (5 cm / 2 inches) ·
2 dessert spoons (1¼ Tbsp) vodka · 10 cl (½ cup) table cream · 1 small bunch
of chives · 2 dessert spoons (1¼ Tbsp) veal bouillon powder · Tabasco sauce ·
salt · freshly ground pepper

In a saucepan, dilute the veal bouillon in 75 cl (3¼ cups) of boiling water. Lower the heat,
simmer for 5 minutes while stirring, and leave to cool. Peel and shred the radish. Slice the
trout into strips.

Using a blender, combine the radish, trout, cream, and cold veal bouillon. Add a little salt,
pepper, and a few drops of Tabasco sauce. Blend until the mixture is smooth and creamy.
Place in the refrigerator for at least 2 hours.

Just before serving, add the vodka and stir well. Divide the soup equally into glasses,
garnish with some chopped chives, and serve chilled.

SUGGESTED WINE PAIRING: a chablis

cream of cauliflower soup with trout roe

EASY AND AFFORDABLE - PREPARATION: 10 MIN - COOKING TIME: 20 MIN

SERVES 6

1 small cauliflower • 50 g (1¾ oz) trout or salmon roe • 15 cl (⅔ cup) table cream • 2 chicken bouillon cubes • salt • freshly ground pepper

Wash the cauliflower, remove the stalk, and detach the florets. Boil 70 cl (3 cups) of water in a saucepan, dilute the bouillon cubes, and add the florets. Leave to simmer for 20 minutes.

Using a blender, mix the cauliflower with the bouillon and the cream. Season with salt and pepper.

Divide the cream of cauliflower soup into bowls and garnish with the trout or salmon roe. Serve warm or cold.

SUGGESTED WINE PAIRING: a white pernand-vergelesses

creative
soups

button mushrooms

Mushrooms are widely consumed in France and are an integral part of French gastronomy. The most popular and easiest to find in France are button mushrooms, commonly known as "champignons de Paris" (Paris mushrooms), which are cultivated mushrooms that grow all year long but require specific climatic and environmental conditions for optimal growth. Indeed, they are grown in the dark, mainly in basements, and often in trays containing natural, fermented, pasteurized compost and mycelium (which consists of very fine filaments that come from tiny single-celled spores – the reproductive parts of fungi).

nutritional benefits

Extremely rich in water, button mushrooms are very low in calories, with only 14 calories per 100 g (3½ oz). They are rich in copper and contain a significant amount of fiber. Particularly nutritious, they are a source of several vitamins and minerals such as copper, selenium, vitamins B2 and B3, pantothenic acid, and vitamin D.

choosing and using

First of all, they have to be carefully selected. Choose mushrooms with a completely closed cap, which is a sign that they are very fresh. Store them in the crisper compartment of the refrigerator for no more than two or three days.

You can also use canned or frozen mushrooms, which only have a slightly lower amount of nutrients than fresh mushrooms.

They can be served raw in salads, together with some herbs and a little vinaigrette. They are delicious in omelets, quiches, etc.

They can also be served as an appetizer: remove the stalks, fill the caps with some creamy herb cheese, sprinkle with breadcrumbs, and bake in the oven for about 15 minutes.

cream of mushroom and walnut soup

EASY AND REASONABLE - PREPARATION : 20 MIN - COOKING TIME : 15 MIN

SERVES 4

500 g (1 lb) button mushrooms • 100 g (3½ oz) fresh porcini mushrooms • 2 shallots • 20 g (¾ oz) walnut kernels • 2 chicken bouillon cubes • 15 cl (⅔ cup) sour heavy cream • 20 g (¾ oz) butter • 1 dessert spoon (2 tsp) walnut oil • salt • freshly ground pepper

Cut off the earthy mushroom stalks. Rapidly wash the mushrooms under cold, running water. Wipe dry with a cloth and thinly slice.

Peel and chop the shallots. Crush the walnut kernels. Dilute the bouillon cubes in 1 L (4 cups) of boiling water.

Heat the butter in a frying pan and sauté the mushrooms. Season with salt and pepper. As soon as the water has evaporated, remove them from the pan, set aside, and brown the shallots in the same pan.

Using a blender or food processor, mix the mushrooms, shallots, cream, and hot bouillon until the texture is light and smooth, like a mousse. Divide the soup into bowls, drizzle with the walnut oil, and sprinkle with the crushed walnuts. Serve piping hot.

SUGGESTED WINE PAIRING : a red bergerac

cream of lentil and chanterelle mushroom soup

EASY AND REASONABLE - PREPARATION: 20 MIN - COOKING TIME: 30 MIN

SERVES 4

200 g (7 oz) small chanterelle mushrooms • 200 g (7 oz) green lentils • 2 shallots • 10 cl (½ cup) very cold UHT table cream • 2 chicken bouillon cubes • 1 dessert spoon (2 tsp) oil • 1 bunch of mixed herbs • whipped cream • salt • freshly ground pepper

Place the lentils in a large saucepan of cold water. Bring to a boil and cook for 5 minutes. Drain, then return the lentils to the saucepan. Add 1.5 L (6 cups) of cold water, the mixed herbs, and the crumbled bouillon cubes. Bring to a boil and simmer for 20 minutes.

Whip the cold cream until stiff and place in the refrigerator. Mix the lentils with their cooking juices until the mixture is smooth and creamy. Season with salt and pepper and keep warm.

Trim the stalks and rapidly wash the mushrooms under cold, running water. Pat dry with a paper towel. Peel and chop the shallots.

Heat the oil in a frying pan and sauté the chanterelle mushrooms with the shallots for 10 minutes over a low heat. Season with salt and pepper and stir well.

Pour the lentil soup into individual bowls. Spread some whipped cream over the top and garnish with the mushrooms. Serve immediately.

SUGGESTED WINE PAIRING: a red baux-de-provence

cream of mushroom soup pies

EASY AND ECONOMICAL - PREPARATION: 15 MIN - CHILLING TIME: 30 MIN
COOKING TIME: 45 MIN

SERVES 4

1 sheet of puff pastry • 1 kg (2¼ lb) button mushrooms • 2 dessert spoons (1¼ Tbsp) veal bouillon powder • 10 cl (½ cup) heavy cream • 15 g (½ oz) butter • 1 onion • 1 bunch of flat-leaf parsley • 1 egg yolk • salt • freshly ground pepper

Clean and chop the mushrooms with a knife. Peel, slice, and sauté the onion in a casserole dish with the butter. Add the mushrooms and cook for 5 minutes. Sprinkle with the veal bouillon powder, add 80 cl (3½ cups) of water, season with salt and pepper, and simmer for 20 minutes. Meanwhile, finely chop the parsley.

Add the heavy cream to the ingredients in the casserole dish and mix until smooth and creamy. Divide the soup into 4 individual ramekins or small, ovenproof bowls. Leave to cool and sprinkle with parsley.

Cut out 4 discs in the puff pastry that are a little larger than the diameter of the bowls or ramekins. Brush the edges with the beaten egg yolk, place the discs on top of the bowls and squeeze the edges so they stick to the sides of the bowls. Brush the pastry lid with the remaining egg yolk. Place the soup bowls for at least 30 minutes in the refrigerator.

Preheat the oven to 210°C (410°F). Place the chilled soup bowls in the oven for about 20 minutes (the dough should puff up and turn golden brown). Serve immediately.

SUGGESTED WINE PAIRING: a corbières rosé

light and creamy chestnut and mushroom soup

A LITTLE EXPENSIVE BUT EASY · PREPARATION: 20 MIN · COOKING TIME: 35 MIN

SERVES 4

500 g (1 lb) peeled chestnuts (fresh, canned, frozen, or vacuum-packed) · 400 g (14 oz) fresh porcini mushrooms · 40 cl (1¾ cups) evaporated milk · 1 dessert spoon (2 tsp) veal bouillon powder · 50 g (1¾ oz) walnut kernels · 2 shallots · 40 g (1½ oz) butter · 2 dessert spoons (1¼ Tbsp) walnut oil · 4 sprigs of chervil · salt · freshly ground pepper

Coarsely chop and rapidly dry roast the walnuts in a nonstick frying pan. Leave to cool on a paper towel.

Pour the evaporated milk into a saucepan, add 40 cl (1¾ cups) of water and the veal bouillon. Bring to a boil while stirring, then add the chestnuts. Season with salt and pepper. Adjust the heat and leave the liquid to simmer for 25 minutes.

Peel and thinly slice the shallots. Clean the mushrooms and cut into strips. Heat the butter in a pan, add the shallots, and sauté gently. Add the mushrooms and brown while stirring over a high heat.

Using an electric or hand blender, mix the chestnuts and their cooking juices until the mixture is smooth and foamy. Check the seasoning, divide the soup into bowls, and top with the golden brown porcini mushrooms. Sprinkle with the chopped chervil and crushed walnuts and drizzle with some walnut oil. Serve immediately.

SUGGESTED WINE PAIRING: a white côtes du jura

CVF RECOMMENDATION: when out of season, use 40 g (1½ oz) dried porcini mushrooms. Soak for 30 minutes in warm water before cooking.

root vegetable bouillon with foie gras

EASY AND REASONABLE - PREPARATION: 30 MIN - COOKING TIME: 50 MIN
RESTING TIME: 2 H

SERVES 4

1 raw chioggia beet • 1 raw yellow beet • 3 carrots • 100 g (3½ oz) shimeji
mushrooms • 200 g (7 oz) uncooked foie gras • 3 lemongrass stalks, divided •
1 kaffir lime • 1 scallion (green onion) • 2 sprigs of cilantro • 2 chicken bouillon
cubes • 1 dessert spoon (2 tsp) olive oil • celery salt • sea salt (fleur de sel) •
Sichuan pepper

Season the foie gras with the sea salt and ground pepper. Wrap it in plastic wrap and place
in the refrigerator for 2 hours. Wash the beets and steam for 45 minutes. Allow to cool then
peel. Cut them into thin round slices and halve each slice.

Remove the outer leaf and the hard ends of the lemongrass and slice in half lengthwise.
Peel and thinly slice the onion. In a stewpot, bring 1 L (4 cups) of water to a boil. Add
2 lemongrass stalks and dilute the bouillon cubes. Peel and cut the carrots into round,
0.2 cm (¹⁄₁₆ inch) thick slices.

Cut the third lemongrass stalk into sections and clean the mushrooms. Heat the oil in a
frying pan, add the lemongrass, beets, carrots, and mushrooms. Brown for 1 minute then
remove from the heat. Season with the celery salt and add the cilantro sprigs.

Cut the foie gras into small, thin slivers and place in the soup bowls. Add the vegetables
and pour the bouillon over the top. Sprinkle with the zest of the kaffir lime and serve
immediately.

SUGGESTED WINE PAIRING: a chablis

cream of porcini mushroom soup with duck breast

EASY AND REASONABLE · PREPARATION: 25 MIN · COOKING TIME: 25 MIN

SERVES 4

75 g (2⅔ oz) dried porcini mushrooms · 3 shallots · 100 g (3½ oz) sliced smoked duck breast · 25 g (⅞ oz) rice flour · 1 celery stalk · 2 cl (4 tsp) port wine · 4 chicken bouillon cubes · 50 g (1¾ oz) butter, divided · salt · freshly ground pepper

Place the mushrooms in a bowl of warm water. Drain. Peel and finely chop the shallots and cook in 30 g (1 oz) of melted butter until soft. Thinly slice the mushrooms (set aside a few for later), add to the frying pan and brown for 1 to 2 minutes, while stirring.

Dilute the bouillon cubes in 1 L (4 cups) of boiling water. Mix the rice flour with a little cold water and stir the chicken bouillon into the rice flour mixture. Add mixture to the porcini mushrooms and bring to a boil. Slice the celery into small sticks and add to the bouillon. Cook for 20 minutes over a low heat and blend. Add the port wine and 20 g (¾ oz) of butter. Season with salt and pepper. Keep warm.

In a frying pan, dry roast the duck breast slices until crisp. Divide the leftover porcini mushroom slices into warm bowls. Pour the soup over the mushrooms and add the duck breast slices. Serve immediately.

SUGGESTED WINE PAIRING: a madiran

garlic, onions and company

Members of the allium family include leeks, onions, shallots, and garlic. Rich in vitamins, minerals, and fiber, they are popular and widely used ingredients, despite the fact that they can cause halitosis (bad breath).

nutritional benefits

Rich in water, allium plants are low in calories with an average of 30 calories per 100 g (3½ oz). They have many virtues: given their high water content, they are natural diuretics. Rich in potassium, they help dilute uric acid, and stimulate the kidneys to eliminate excess amounts from the body through urine. The draining effect is particularly obvious with garlic, onions, and leeks.

Often associated with folk remedies because of their high sulfur content, garlic onions and shallots have been used for many years in natural medicine to treat intestinal, urinary, and lung infections, or small infections, with the use of cataplasms. Allium foods have also been recognized as agents for the prevention of cardiovascular diseases and cancer, thanks to their high level of antioxidants.

choosing and using

Although they are mostly used to season food, some can be used as vegetables. By simply cutting them into thin slices and cooking slowly, you can make onion or shallot jam, a leek fondue or a confit of garlic cloves.

They can also be the main ingredient of a dish. For example, scoop out the inside of some large red onions, fill them with a mixture of minced meat, herbs, and egg, and you have a traditional, Mediterranean dish from Nice known as "les petits farcis" (little stuffed vegetables). You can also use onions in soups and tarts.

Leeks can be steamed and served cold with a mild, mustard-based vinaigrette. They add flavor to sauces and slow-cooked dishes but are also delicious raw, or in steak tartare, carpaccio, hamburgers, etc. They are more nutritious when eaten raw but more easily digestible when cooked.

Lautrec pink garlic soup

EASY AND ECONOMICAL - PREPARATION: 15 MIN - COOKING TIME: 15 MIN

SERVES 4

10 cloves of pink garlic • 2 chicken bouillon cubes • 8 slices of French bread

For the mayonnaise: 1 egg yolk • ½ dessert spoon (1 tsp) mustard • 15 cl
(⅔ cup) olive oil • salt • freshly ground pepper • 1 pinch of Espelette pepper

Prepare the mayonnaise: in a bowl, mix the egg yolk, mustard, salt, pepper, and Espelette pepper. Slowly pour in the oil while whisking, until the mixture thickens and resembles a mayonnaise.

Peel and crush the garlic with a mortar and pestle. Bring 1.5 L (6 cups) of salted water to a boil in a stewpot, add the garlic and bouillon cubes, stir, and simmer for 10 minutes.

Toast the slices of French bread. Add a ladle of bouillon to the mayonnaise, then pour the contents of the bowl into the stewpot, stir, and turn off the heat.

Pour the soup into bowls and serve immediately with the slices of toasted French bread.

SUGGESTED WINE PAIRING: a côtes de provence rosé

vegetable bouillabaisse with eggs

EASY AND ECONOMICAL - PREPARATION: 10 MIN - COOKING TIME: 20 MIN

SERVES 6

6 eggs • 300 g (10 oz) potatoes • 2 tomatoes • 1 leek • 4 garlic cloves •
1 onion • ¼ fennel bulb • 2 pinches of saffron powder • 1 strip of orange zest •
2 dessert spoons (1¼ Tbsp) olive oil • salt • freshly ground pepper • 6 slices of
toasted bread rubbed with garlic

Scald the tomatoes for 10 seconds. Peel, seed, and cut them into cubes. Peel the onion,
leek, garlic, and potatoes. Chop the onion and garlic separately, cut the leek into round
slices, and cut the potatoes into large cubes. Thinly slice the fennel with a knife.

Pour the olive oil into a stewpot and cook the onion, leek, and fennel until soft. Add the
tomatoes, garlic, orange zest, and saffron, and season with salt and pepper. Add 1.5 L
(6 cups) of water and simmer for 15 minutes.

Just before serving, break the eggs one by one into a cup and carefully add to the bouillon.
Poach for 4 minutes in the simmering (not boiling) bouillon. Serve immediately with toasted
bread rubbed with garlic.

SUGGESTED WINE PAIRING: a côtes de provence rosé

chicken consommé with ravioli

EASY AND ECONOMICAL · PREPARATION: 15 MIN · COOKING TIME: 30 MIN

SERVES 6

240 g (8½ oz) "ravioles de Royans" (tiny ravioli filled with a blend of cheese and herbs – frozen or fresh) · 4 low fat chicken bouillon cubes · 450 g (16 oz) frozen julienne vegetables · 2 dessert spoons (1¼ Tbsp) soy sauce · 6 sprigs of chervil · 2 very fresh egg yolks · juice of 1 lemon · 20 g (¾ oz) butter

Melt the butter in a frying pan. Add the julienne vegetables and, stirring regularly, cook until soft but not brown. At the same time, in a large saucepan, bring 1.6 L (6¾ cups) of water to a boil with the crumbled bouillon cubes. Allow to simmer for 10 minutes then add the soy sauce and leave to simmer for another 5 minutes.

Meanwhile, whisk the egg yolks and lemon juice in a mixing bowl. Add a ladle of hot bouillon, whisk briskly, and set aside. Separate the ravioli and immerse in the bouillon with the julienne vegetables. Cook for 2 minutes.

Turn off the heat and pour the contents of the mixing bowl over the ravioli. Stir gently, then divide the soup into bowls, garnish with the chervil sprigs, and serve immediately.

SUGGESTED WINE PAIRING: a white côtes de gascogne

creamy pea soup with quinoa sprouts

QUITE EASY AND ECONOMICAL · PREPARATION: 35 MIN · COOKING TIME: 25 MIN

SERVES 4

1 kg (2¼ lb) fresh peas · 4 chicken bouillon cubes · 1 onion · 100 g (3½ oz) heavy sour cream · 4 dessert spoons (2¾ Tbsp) quinoa sprouts · butter · salt · freshly ground pepper

Shell the peas. Peel and chop the onion. Melt a little butter in a casserole dish and add the onion.

Stir constantly and cook for about 3 minutes over a low heat until transparent. Dilute the bouillon cubes in 1 L (4 cups) of water and add the peas. Season with salt and pepper and cook for about 20 minutes, until the peas are tender.

Blend the peas with an immersion blender, sift out excess liquid, and pour back into the casserole dish. Bring back to a boil and add the sour cream.

Serve in individual bowls and top each with 1 dessert spoon (2 tsp) of quinoa, just before serving.

SUGGESTED WINE PAIRING: a provence rosé

chicken and tomato soup

EASY AND ECONOMICAL - PREPARATION: 10 MIN - COOKING TIME: 40 MIN

SERVES 4
1 bottle of Passata la Rossa with vegetables (cream of tomato soup with vegetables) • 2 chicken legs • 1 dessert spoon (2 tsp) mascarpone • a few celery leaves • salt • freshly ground pepper

Pour 1 L (4 cups) of water and the tomato soup into a large saucepan. Add the chicken and salt, and cover. Simmer for about 40 minutes, until the chicken is very tender.

Drain the chicken, remove the skin and bones, and shred the flesh.

Add the mascarpone to the soup and stir well. Divide the soup into bowls, add the chicken, top with the celery leaves and season with pepper. Serve immediately.

SUGGESTED WINE PAIRING: a provence rosé

healthy
soups

squash

Squash is the generic term for the fruit of the Cucurbita genus and Cucurbitaceae family, which are considered as vegetables and cooked as such. There are dozens of varieties, the best known being pumpkins, butternut squash, and acorn squash.

nutritional benefits

Rich in water (about 92 percent of the fruit), squash is low in calories with about 25 calories per 100 g (3½ oz). It is an excellent source of antioxidants, beta carotene, and vitamins, mainly vitamin A. It also contains iron and copper. Furthermore, it is rich in dietary fiber, with about 1.5 g (0.05 oz) of fibers per 100 g (3½ oz) of flesh, and minerals, including potassium. The low level of sodium in squash is another of its health benefits.

choosing and using

Store squash at room temperature and not in the refrigerator, which makes vegetables too moist. Squash is very suitable for freezing – simply cut it into large cubes before placing in the freezer.

Squash can be cooked in different ways: peel and cut the squash into large cubes and place in an ovenproof dish. Drizzle with olive oil and sprinkle with herbs.

Butternut squash is delicious in soups with a little cream, or puréed.

Invent new versions of stuffed vegetables by filling small varieties of squash with a mixture of minced meat, herbs, cheese . . .

Squash has a slightly sweet taste so try innovating by using it in sweet dishes too, such as cakes, muffins, or even jam!

Consider saving the seeds. Pan roasted, they are delicious and can be served with an aperitif; ground, they can be used in sauces.

pumpkin and beet soup

EASY AND ECONOMICAL - PREPARATION: 20 MIN - COOKING TIME: 35 MIN

SERVES 6

1.2 kg (2½ lb) pumpkin • 200 g (7 oz) raw beet • 2 white portions of leek • 1 onion • 1 celery stalk • 100 g (3½ oz) grated Swiss cheese • 40 cl (1¾ cups) table cream • 60 g (2 oz) butter • 1 pinch of nutmeg • salt • freshly ground pepper

Peel and dice the onion. Remove the strings from the celery with a vegetable peeler, peel the beet, and clean the leeks. Cut the vegetables into small cubes. Melt 30 g (1 oz) of butter in a saucepan, add the vegetables and onion and slowly cook until soft. Add 1 L (4 cups) of water, season with salt and pepper, and simmer for 30 minutes.

Meanwhile, remove the skin, seeds, and filaments of the pumpkin, and cut the flesh into large cubes.

Heat 30 g (1 oz) of butter in a saucepan, add the pumpkin cubes, and steam slowly for 5 minutes. Season with salt and pepper and add the nutmeg and 50 cl (2 cups) of hot water. Simmer for 20 minutes.

Mix the contents of the 2 saucepans separately and divide the table cream equally between both. Check the seasoning and rectify, if necessary.

Pour both soups into a tureen without stirring. Sprinkle with the grated cheese and a little ground pepper (1 twist of the pepper mill). So that the soup maintains its original, attractive, two-tone aspect, serve immediately.

SUGGESTED WINE PAIRING: a napa valley zinfandel

cream of asparagus soup

EASY AND ECONOMICAL - PREPARATION: 15 MIN - COOKING TIME: 20 MIN

SERVES 4

400 g (14 oz) green asparagus • 4 dessert spoons (2¾ Tbsp) salmon roe,
divided • 35 cl (1½ cups) milk • 25 cl (1 cup) very cold table cream, divided •
4 sprigs of chervil • salt • white pepper

Peel the asparagus from the tip downward and remove the fibrous part at the end of
the stalk. Set aside 1 asparagus tip for the garnish. Cut the other stalks into medium-sized
segments.

Boil 50 cl (2 cups) of water in a saucepan with the milk and half of the cream. Season with
salt and pepper. Once the liquid is boiling, add the asparagus. Cover and cook over a low
heat for 20 minutes.

Meanwhile, whip the remaining cream until it becomes stiff. Season with a little salt, add half
of the salmon roe, and place in the refrigerator. Thinly slice the reserved raw asparagus tip.

Blend the contents of the saucepan until the mixture is smooth and creamy. Divide it equally
into bowls and top with a spoonful of whipped cream. Garnish with the sliced asparagus tip,
the rest of the salmon roe, and a sprig of chervil. Serve immediately.

SUGGESTED WINE PAIRING: a white anjou

fennel, Swiss chard and zucchini soup

EASY AND ECONOMICAL · PREPARATION: 10 MIN · COOKING TIME: 30 MIN

SERVES 4

3 Swiss chard leaves · 1 large fennel bulb · 2 zucchini · 1 onion · 3 dessert
spoons (2 Tbsp) olive oil · 1 L (4 cups) water · coarse gray salt · 2 fennel leaves

Wash and drain the chard leaves, fennel bulb, and zucchini.

In a casserole dish, heat the olive oil and cook the chopped onion until it is transparent. Cut
all the vegetables into large pieces, add them to the casserole dish, and cover with a liter
of water.

Cook over a low heat for 30 minutes until the vegetables are al dente. Season with salt and
coarsely mix. Drizzle with the olive oil and garnish with the finely chopped fennel leaves.

SUGGESTED WINE PAIRING: a white sylvaner

cream of zucchini soup

EASY AND ECONOMICAL - PREPARATION: 10 MIN - COOKING TIME: 20 MIN

SERVES 4

20 g (¾ oz) butter • 1 onion • 500 g (1 lb) small zucchini • 2 chicken bouillon cubes • 4 portions Laughing Cow cheese • salt • pepper

Peel and finely chop the onion. Wash and cut the zucchini into thin round slices. Melt the butter in a casserole dish and add the onion and zucchini slices. Season with salt and pepper and add the crumbled chicken bouillon cubes and 75 cl (3¼ cups) of hot water.

Simmer for 20 minutes, add the 4 portions of Laughing Cow cheese, and mix until the soup is smooth and creamy. Serve immediately in tall, narrow glasses.

SUGGESTED WINE PAIRING: a white côtes de gascogne

lamb's lettuce

amb's lettuce is the quintessential winter lettuce and is very popular with the French. It is at its best from mid-October to May. As a cultivated lettuce, it is a speciality of the Nantes region in France, so much so that lamb's lettuce grown in the area has been granted Protected Geographical Indication (PGI) status.

nutritional benefits

Lamb's lettuce is naturally rich in omega-3 fatty acids, which help prevent coronary heart diseases. It contains as much omega-3 as wild purslane and is widely used in Cretan cuisine.

Its vitamin C content helps improve the absorption of iron. It also contains other antioxidant substances, which help combat cellular aging: vitamin E and provitamin A (beta-carotene). It is an excellent source of vitamin B9 (folic acid), which is necessary for pregnant women, and 100 g (3½ oz) of lamb's lettuce provides 46 percent of the recommended nutritional intake for an adult.

It is also a source of calcium and fiber. As it contains only 14 calories per 100 g (3½ oz), it can be consumed without moderation!

choosing and using

Bought loose, lamb's lettuce needs to be thoroughly washed. When it is sold in a carton, the earth has already been removed so it just needs to be rinsed. Purchased fresh and ready-to-use in a plastic bag, it can be eaten as it is.

Its succulent green leaves are extremely tempting and, as a salad, it is delicious. It can be eaten on its own with just a drizzle of olive, sesame or walnut oil, or with a savory tart, smoked salmon, a scallop carpaccio, or cheese. Mixed with olive oil, salt, pepper, and a handful of walnuts, it makes a very tasty pesto. It is also nice in sandwiches.

Its mild, delicate flavor goes not only very well with beet and walnuts, but also with tangy fruits such a green apple or grapefruit.

It is also delicious cooked. Scalded, cooled, and mixed, it becomes a tasty sauce that can be served with fish. It can replace spinach in cheese puffs or phyllo pastry rolls. Sautéed for a few minutes in olive oil, it becomes an original accompaniment to other dishes, and when cooked and mixed with one or two potatoes, a shallot and a spoonful of cream, it makes a smooth, creamy soup.

cream of lamb's lettuce soup

EASY AND ECONOMICAL - PREPARATION: 15 MIN - COOKING TIME: 20 MIN

SERVES 4

500 g (1 lb) lamb's lettuce • 2 zucchini • 2 shallots • 30 cl (1¼ cups) whole milk • 20 g (¾ oz) butter • salt • freshly ground pepper

Wash and dry the lamb's lettuce. Rinse the zucchini, discard the ends, and cut into round slices. Peel and finely chop the shallots.

Heat the butter in a frying pan and, stirring constantly, sauté the shallots until they are transparent. Add the lamb's lettuce and the zucchini slices. Stir with a wooden spoon for 2 to 3 minutes, then add 30 cl (1¼ cups) of warm water and season with salt. Simmer for 15 minutes. Transfer all the ingredients to a food processor or blender, mix, and set aside.

Just before serving, heat the milk in a saucepan. Mix the soup with the hot milk and some pepper (a few twists of the pepper mill). Serve the soup in a tureen or individual soup bowls.

SUGGESTED WINE PAIRING: an entre-deux-mers

warm herb soup

EASY AND ECONOMICAL - PREPARATION: 20 MIN - COOKING TIME: 30 MIN

SERVES 6

1 bunch of chervil • 1 bunch of basil • 1 bunch of chives • 4 scallions (green onions) • 2 tomatoes • 1 zucchini • 6 very fresh eggs • 12 nasturtium flowers • olive oil • salt • freshly ground pepper

Wash and pat dry the bunches of herbs and discard the thickest stems. Set aside a few sprigs of chervil for garnish. Boil, peel, and seed the tomatoes. Cut the tomato flesh into cubes. Peel the zucchini and also cut into cubes. Peel and thinly slice the onions, then sauté them in a large saucepan with 3 dessert spoons (2 Tbsp) of olive oil. Add the herbs, diced tomatoes, and zucchini. Cook for 5 minutes and add 1.5 L (6 cups) of water. Season with salt and pepper, cover, and simmer for 30 minutes.

Meanwhile, prepare the soft-boiled eggs: boil 1 L (4 cups) of water in a saucepan and, when boiling, carefully add the eggs and cook for 5 minutes. Cool them under cold running water and remove the shells.

When the time is up, mix the soup, allow it to cool, and divide it equally into bowls. Place a soft-boiled egg in the center of each bowl, sprinkle with chervil, and garnish with the nasturtium flowers.

SUGGESTED WINE PAIRING: a dry montlouis-sur-loire

cream of parsley soup with fresh goat cheese dumplings

EASY AND ECONOMICAL - PREPARATION: 20 MIN - COOKING TIME: 15 MIN

SERVES 4

2 bunches of flat-leaf parsley • 150 g (5 oz) celeriac • 2 starchy potatoes •
150 g (5 oz) fresh goat cheese • 2 chicken bouillon cubes • 1 small bunch of
mixed herbs (chervil, chives, tarragon) • 20 cl (¾ cup) light cream • 1 dessert
spoon (2 tsp) olive oil • salt • freshly ground pepper

Peel the celeriac and potatoes and cut them into cubes. In a large saucepan, boil
1.2 L (5 cups) of water with the crumbled bouillon cubes. Add the diced vegetables
and cook for about 15 minutes.

Meanwhile, remove the leaves from the parsley, rinse, and reserve 1 dessert spoon
(2 tsp) of leaves for garnish. Add the other leaves to the bouillon with the vegetables, cook
for 1 minute, then blend all the ingredients until the mixture is smooth and creamy.

Add salt and pepper, check the seasoning, and set aside.

Rinse and finely chop the chervil, chives, and tarragon. In a bowl, mash the goat cheese
with a fork and add the chopped herbs, salt, and pepper. Pour the olive oil into the bowl
and mix thoroughly. Using 2 dessert spoons, shape the goat cheese mixture into oval
dumplings and set aside.

Warm the soup over a low heat and pour into serving bowls. Place the dumplings on top,
add a dash of light cream, and garnish with the parsley leaves. Serve immediately.

SUGGESTED WINE PAIRING: a white sancerre

winter
soups

chestnut soup with smoked duck breast

EASY AND REASONABLE · PREPARATION: 20 MIN · COOKING TIME: 50 MIN

SERVES 4

500 g (1 lb) chestnuts · 1 L (4 cups) milk · 2 tender celery ribs · 100 g (3½ oz) smoked duck breast · 2 dessert spoons (1¼ Tbsp) heavy cream · ½ chicken bouillon cube · grated nutmeg · salt · freshly ground pepper

Make a slit in the flat side of the chestnuts and immerse in boiling water. When the water starts boiling again, cook for 5 minutes. Drain, allow to cool, and peel.

Pour the milk into a saucepan and add the peeled chestnuts. Season with salt and pepper. Slowly bring to a boil over a low heat, partially cover, and cook for 50 minutes, stirring regularly.

Dilute the ½ bouillon cube in 20 cl (¾ cup) of boiling water. Using a food mill (small holes), an electric blender, or food processor, purée the chestnuts. Add the cream, bouillon, and grated nutmeg, and keep warm.

Cut the duck breast into thin strips and dry roast in a nonstick frying pan. Finely chop the celery ribs. Transfer the soup to a tureen or individual bowls. Garnish with the strips of roasted duck and chopped celery. Serve immediately.

SUGGESTED WINE PAIRING: a dry white bergerac

corn and popcorn soup

EASY AND ECONOMICAL · PREPARATION: 25 MIN · COOKING TIME: 40 MIN

SERVES 4

250 g (½ lb) canned sweet corn · 2 small tomatoes · 125 g (4½ oz) diced
smoked bacon (lardons) · 2 shallots · 1 garlic clove · 40 g (1½ oz) popcorn
kernels · 2 chicken bouillon cubes · 25 cl (1 cup) table cream · 2 dessert
spoons (1¼ Tbsp) olive oil · ½ dessert spoon (1 tsp) neutral oil · salt · freshly
ground pepper

Drain the canned corn. Peel and coarsely slice the garlic and shallots. Wash and cut the
tomatoes into cubes.

Pour the neutral oil into a saucepan. Add the popcorn kernels, cover, and place over a very
high heat while shaking the saucepan. When the corn has finished "popping," remove the
saucepan from the heat, season with salt, stir, and set aside.

Heat the olive oil in a casserole dish and brown the bacon over a high heat. Drain with a
skimmer and place on a paper towel. Place the casserole dish with the melted bacon fat
back over the heat. Brown the shallots and garlic, then add the drained sweet corn and the
tomatoes. Stir for 3 minutes over a medium heat, then add 1 L (4 cups) of boiling water.
Add the bouillon cubes and leave to simmer for 20 minutes.

After 20 minutes, add the cream and cook for another 10 minutes. Use an electric or hand
blender to mix the soup and blend until it is smooth and creamy.

Divide the bacon and popcorn equally into individual bowls, cover with the soup, season
with pepper, and serve immediately.

SUGGESTED WINE PAIRING: a condrieu

French tartiflette soup

EASY AND ECONOMICAL · PREPARATION: 15 MIN · COOKING TIME: 30 MIN

SERVES 4

½ Reblochon farm cheese · 6 large ordinary potatoes · ¼ celeriac bulb ·
200 g (7 oz) smoked diced bacon (lardons) · 1 onion · 60 cl (2½ cups) milk ·
20 cl (¾ cup) table cream · nutmeg · salt · freshly ground pepper

Peel the potatoes and celery and cut into cubes. Peel and chop the onion. Boil the
milk and cream in a large saucepan, add the potatoes, celery, and onion. Simmer for
20 minutes.

When the time is up, season with salt, pepper, and 1 pinch of nutmeg, and mix to obtain a
smooth, creamy mixture. Pour the soup back into the saucepan over a very low heat.

Remove the rind from the Reblochon and cut the cheese into small pieces. Add it to the
soup and leave to melt, stirring occasionally. Meanwhile, dry roast the diced bacon in a
frying pan.

When the soup is smooth and creamy, divide it into individual bowls, sprinkle with the
bacon, and serve immediately.

SUGGESTED WINE PAIRING: a chablis

leek, potato and fennel soup

EASY AND ECONOMICAL - PREPARATION: 10 MIN - COOKING TIME: 30 MIN

SERVES 6
6 leeks • 1 celery stalk • 4 starchy potatoes • 2 chicken bouillon cubes •
½ dessert spoon (1 tsp) fennel seeds • 3 dessert spoons (2 Tbsp) heavy
cream • 30 g (1 oz) butter • salt • freshly ground pepper

Peel the leeks and discard two-thirds of the green part. Cut them into thin slices and wash
several times. Remove the strings from the celery stalk and slice. Peel, wash, and cut the
potatoes into cubes.

Melt the butter in a casserole dish and brown the fennel seeds for 5 minutes while stirring.
Set some seeds aside for garnish. Transfer the potatoes, leeks, and celery to the casserole
dish. Season with salt and pepper and brown for 5 minutes. Add 1.2 L (5 cups) of water
and the crumbled bouillon cubes. Stir and leave to simmer for 20 minutes.

After 20 minutes, add the heavy cream and purée the soup in a food mill, electric blender,
or with a hand blender.

Divide the soup into bowls, garnish with the reserved golden fennel seeds, and serve
piping hot.

SUGGESTED WINE PAIRING: a saint-péray

vegetable and pasta minestrone

QUITE EASY AND ECONOMICAL - PREPARATION: 20 MIN - COOKING TIME: 30 TO 40 MIN

SERVES 6

2 carrots • 1 celery stalk • 200 g (7 oz) celeriac bulb • 200 g (7 oz) parsnip •
½ bunch of scallions • 200 g (7 oz) rutabaga • 200 g (7 oz) turnips • 5 turnip-
rooted chervil roots • 1 garlic clove • ½ bunch of flat-leaf parsley • 1.5 L
(6 cups) instant chicken bouillon • 1 very small bunch of mixed herbs (thyme,
bay leaf, sprigs of parsley) • 50 g (1¾ oz) penne pasta • 2 slices of nut bread •
4 slices of speck ham • 4 dessert spoons (2¾ Tbsp) olive oil, divided • salt •
freshly ground pepper

Peel, wash, and dice the root vegetables. Wash and finely chop the celery. Peel and chop
the scallions, keeping some of their green. Peel the garlic, remove the germ, and crush the
clove.

Heat 2 dessert spoons (1¼ Tbsp) of olive oil in a stewpot, add the onions and garlic, fry
for 2 minutes, then add the other vegetables (except for the chervil). Season with salt and
pepper and cook for 3 minutes. Add the bouillon and the bunch of mixed herbs. Leave to
simmer for 20 minutes.

Brown the bread slices in a frying pan with the remaining olive oil. Wash the parsley,
remove the leaves, and finely chop. Add the pasta, parsley, and chervil to the minestrone,
and simmer until the pasta is tender (4 to 10 minutes).

Serve the vegetables in their hot bouillon with small slivers of speck ham and nut
bread croutons.

SUGGESTED WINE PAIRING: a mont-louis blanc

creamy navy bean soup with smoked duck breast and truffle oil

EASY AND REASONABLE - PREPARATION: 20 MIN - COOKING TIME: 50 MIN

SERVES 4

1.5 kg (3 lb) fresh Paimpol navy beans • 8 slices of smoked duck breast •
1 carrot • 1 onion • 1 bunch of mixed herbs • 10 cl (½ cup) whole table cream •
3 cl (⅛ cup) truffle oil • 1 chicken bouillon cube • salt • Espelette pepper

Shell the beans. Peel and finely slice the onion and carrot. Place the beans in a stewpot and add the onion, carrot, a little salt, and the bunch of mixed herbs. Cover with 2 L (8 cups) of cold water. Add the crumbled bouillon cube and bring to a boil. Cover the stewpot, reduce the heat, and cook over a low heat for 45 minutes.

Shred the slices of duck breast and dry roast until brown in a nonstick frying pan.

Once the beans are cooked, remove the mixed herbs, add the cream, and mix all the ingredients with a hand blender. Warm the soup for a few minutes then pour into individual soup bowls.

Garnish with the shredded duck, drizzle with the truffle oil, and season with a small pinch of Espelette pepper. Serve immediately.

SUGGESTED WINE PAIRING: a cahors

pumpkin soup with chestnuts
and black pudding

QUITE EASY AND ECONOMICAL - PREPARATION: 15 MIN - COOKING TIME: 35 MIN

SERVES 4

800 g (1¾ lb) pumpkin • 400 g (14 oz) peeled sweet chestnuts, divided •
12 slices of black sausage • 1 celery stalk • 1 onion • 1 L (4 cups) milk •
20 cl (¾ cup) table cream • 50 g (1¾ oz) butter, divided • salt • freshly
ground pepper

Peel the pumpkin, remove the seeds and filaments, and cut the flesh into cubes. Remove
the strings from the celery stalk and cut into sections. Peel and finely chop the onion. Melt
30 g (1 oz) of butter in a casserole dish. Add the onion, pumpkin, and celery, cover and
steam for about ten minutes.

Set aside 8 whole chestnuts and place the others in the casserole dish. Add the milk,
season with salt and pepper, bring to a boil while stirring, then lower the heat and leave
to simmer for 20 minutes. Meanwhile, finely slice the 8 remaining chestnuts with a sharp
knife.

Fry the slices of black sausage in the remaining butter for 5 minutes. Drain and keep
warm. In the same pan, lightly brown the chestnut slices over a medium heat.

Mix the contents of the casserole dish while slowly adding the cream until the mixture is
smooth. Divide the soup equally into serving bowls and add 3 slices of sausage to each
bowl. Garnish with the chestnut "chips" and serve piping hot.

SUGGESTED WINE PAIRING: a white meursault

gourmet
soups

endives

Discovered by chance in the nineteenth century by the head of the Botanical Garden of Brussels, the endive, also known as the chicory in certain countries, has many peculiarities. First of all, it requires a hot and humid atmosphere and a total absence of sunlight to prevent its leaves from turning green and opening up. This explains why it is not found in the wild. Indeed, in the open air, the endive root only produces one flower. The seeds are sown in May and they form cultivated roots like carrots. The roots are harvested between September and November and placed in cellars to grow into endives. They are sold without their roots, peeled, sorted, and packaged, and can be found practically all year round.

nutritional benefits

The endive is composed of nearly 95 percent water with only 15 calories per 100 g (3½ oz). It is low in fat but rich in fiber with 2 to 2.5 g (⅒ oz) per 100 g (3½ oz), making it an ideal ingredient when on a diet. It is an excellent source of minerals, including potassium, phosphorus, calcium, and magnesium, which is required for energy production, especially during the long winter months.

It is also a source of many trace elements: it supplies 10 percent of the recommended daily intake of selenium, which protects the cells from aging. Finally, the endive is also rich in vitamin C, B1, and B2.

choosing and using

There is no need to wash them. All you have to do is remove the outer leaves and cut off the stalk at the base. For less bitterness, remove the hard cone (with a sharp knife). Endives can be prepared in many different ways:

- Steamed for 10 minutes, pan fried for 25 minutes, boiled in water for 20 minutes, braised for 25 minutes, or even cooked in the microwave for 5 to 10 minutes.

- Before cooking, spray them with a little lemon juice so they stay white.

- Try replacing traditional canapés with an endive leaf as the base, which you can spread with a mixture of crab, avocado, and mayonnaise.

- They are delicious served with sautéed wild mushrooms topped with thin slices of cheese.

- Traditional dishes like ham and endive cheese gratins are always very popular, but try serving them as a side dish. Braised with honey and spices or served like a tarte tatin, caramelized endives are sure to be a success!

They can also be used in soups with some heavy sour cream, and their slightly bitter flavor goes very well with a nice cut of grilled meat.

crayfish tartare with endive cappuccino

A LITTLE TRICKY AND A LITTLE EXPENSIVE - PREPARATION : 30 MIN - COOKING TIME : 35 MIN

SERVES 4

16 raw crayfish • 4 sea urchins • 1 dessert spoon (2 tsp) olive oil • 4 sprigs of tarragon • 10 cl (½ cup) very cold table cream • peel from ¼ of a grapefruit • peel from ¼ of a lemon • zest from ¼ of an orange • 250 g (½ lb) granulated sugar

For the cappuccino: 4 endives • 1 large onion • 10 cl (½ cup) dry white wine • 2 chicken bouillon cubes • 15 cl (⅔ cup) heavy cream • 1 dessert spoon (2 tsp) duck fat • 1 pinch of Espelette pepper • 2 pinches of sugar • salt

Cut the peels of the citrus fruits into very thin julienne strips. Add the 250 g (½ lb) of sugar to 50 cl (2 cups) of water and bring to a boil. Add the peels and zest to the syrup and cook for 20 minutes in the simmering liquid.

Meanwhile, for the cappuccino, peel and chop the onion and clean and cut the endives into pieces. Dilute the bouillon cubes in 70 cl (3 cups) of hot water. Heat the duck fat in a casserole dish, add the onion and endives, and sauté, without browning, over a low heat. Add the wine, bouillon, and heavy cream. Season with salt and pepper, add 2 pinches of sugar, stir, and leave to simmer for 15 minutes.

Peel the crayfish by opening the shell along the underside with scissors. Set aside 4 whole crayfish for garnish. Chop the other crayfish with a knife. Using scissors, cut open the sea urchins horizontally, remove the coral with a small spoon and set aside.

Drain the zests, chop, and add to the chopped crayfish. Stir, bind with the olive oil, add some chopped tarragon, and stir again.

Place an equal amount of crayfish tartare and sea urchin coral in the center of 4 soup bowls. Whip the cold cream until it is stiff. Mix the contents of the casserole dish until the mixture is smooth and creamy. Pour the piping hot soup over the tartare and corals, halve the remaining crayfish and add as garnish, add a touch of whipped cream and a few sprigs of tarragon, and serve immediately.

SUGGESTED WINE PAIRING : a white côtes de saint-mont

cream of celery soup with oysters

EASY AND REASONABLE - PREPARATION: 15 MIN - COOKING TIME: 50 MIN

SERVES 6

30 large cupped oysters • 1 kg (2¼ lb) celeriac bulbs • 1 small celery heart •
20 cl (¾ cup) milk • 25 cl (1 cup) table cream • 50 g (1¾ oz) caviar (optional) •
salt • freshly ground pepper

Peel the celeriac bulb and cut into large cubes. Finely chop the celery and set aside the
leaves for the garnish. Steam the celeriac cubes and chopped celery for 40 minutes until
very soft. Purée the mixture with a food processor and season with salt. Add the milk and
blend again for a few seconds. Pour the celery soup into a saucepan and set aside.

Shuck the oysters and remove them from their shells. Strain the oyster liquid into a
saucepan and briefly boil. Add the oysters and poach for 30 seconds, then remove the
saucepan from the heat.

Warm the cream of celery soup over a low heat, season with pepper, and pour into
individual soup bowls. Place the oysters on top of the soup, garnish with the celery leaves,
and possibly a little caviar. Serve immediately.

SUGGESTED WINE PAIRING: a chablis

cream of leek soup with oysters

EASY AND REASONABLE - PREPARATION : 30 MIN - COOKING TIME : 20 MIN

SERVES 4

16 oysters (n°4) • 4 small leeks • 1 zucchini • 2 chicken bouillon cubes •
¼ dessert spoon (½ tsp) curry powder • 15 cl (⅔ cup) heavy sour cream •
2 dessert spoons (1¼ Tbsp) oil • 8 sprigs of cilantro • salt • freshly ground
pepper

Prepare the bouillon in a large saucepan by diluting the bouillon cubes in 80 cl
(3½ cups) of boiling water. Wash the vegetables and cut the leeks into sections (set aside
6 strips for garnish). Discard the ends of the zucchini, peel (but leave some green), and cut
into thin round slices.

Place the vegetables in the saucepan with the curry and cilantro.

Meanwhile, shuck the oysters, collect the liquid, remove the shells, and set aside. Strain
the oyster liquid. Using a paper towel, pat dry the 6 leek strips then cook for a few minutes
in a nonstick frying pan with the oil. Remove from the pan with a skimming ladle and place
on a paper towel.

Mix the vegetables, add the cream and oyster liquid, and heat for a few minutes. Divide the
soup into 4 bowls, add the oysters, and garnish with the leek strips, salt and pepper. Serve
immediately.

SUGGESTED WINE PAIRING : a sylvaner

cream of lentil soup with marinated salmon

EASY AND REASONABLE - PREPARATION: 10 MIN - COOKING TIME: 45 MIN

SERVES 4

200 g (7 oz) green Puy lentils • 400 g (14 oz) marinated salmon • 2 carrots •
1 celery stalk + 1 small heart • 2 garlic cloves • 15 cl (⅔ cup) table cream •
1 dessert spoon (2 tsp) olive oil • salt • freshly ground pepper • 4 thin slices of
toasted bread

Clean the carrots and celery stalk and place them in a casserole dish. Add the lentils,
peeled garlic, and 1 L (4 cups) of water. Bring to a boil, cover, and simmer for
45 minutes over a low heat.

Remove a small ladle of cooked lentils from the dish, drain, and set aside. Pour the rest
of the warm lentils and their cooking juices into a food processor (or you can use a hand
blender) and purée.

Transfer the purée to the casserole dish, add the reserved lentils, pour in the cream,
season with salt and pepper, stir, and warm over a low heat. Meanwhile, thinly slice the
salmon and celery heart.

Divide the hot, creamy lentil soup and salmon slices into bowls. Drizzle with a few drops
of oil and garnish with the celery. Serve immediately with thin slices of toast and freshly
ground pepper.

SUGGESTED WINE PAIRING: a dry jurançon

cream of asparagus soup with crayfish

EASY AND REASONABLE - PREPARATION: 35 MIN - COOKING TIME: 1 H

SERVES 6

12 crayfish • 1 kg (2¼ lb) green asparagus • 3 shallots • 2 chicken bouillon cubes • 60 g (2 oz) butter, divided • 2 dessert spoons (1¼ Tbsp) olive oil • 10 cl (½ cup) dry white wine • flat-leaf parsley • chervil • 1 dessert spoon (2 tsp) heavy sour cream • salt • freshly ground pepper

Peel the crayfish. Place the tails in the refrigerator and cook the heads and shells in a frying pan with the oil until they change color. Add the white wine and reduce by two-thirds. Add 1 L (4 cups) of boiling water and the bouillon cubes. Season with salt and pepper. Cook for 20 minutes over a low heat.

Strain the bouillon through a fine mesh sieve. Squeeze the shells hard in order to recover a maximum of liquid before discarding them.

Peel the asparagus and cut off the tips. Peel and thinly slice the shallots. Melt 30 g (1 oz) of butter in a saucepan. Sauté the shallots, asparagus stalks, and chopped parsley. Cook for 5 minutes. Add the bouillon, cover, and simmer for 30 minutes. Mix the ingredients with a food processor and keep warm.

Meanwhile, pan fry the asparagus tips in the remaining butter for 5 minutes. Add the crayfish tails and cook for 2 minutes. Season with salt and pepper. Transfer the asparagus and crayfish to the soup. Divide into bowls and garnish with the sprigs of chervil and cream. Serve warm.

SUGGESTED WINE PAIRING: a white saint-joseph

creamy black sausage soup with lobster

A LITTLE EXPENSIVE BUT EASY · PREPARATION: 10 MIN · COOKING TIME: 5 MIN

SERVES 4

400 g (14 oz) black sausage · 1 lobster cooked in a court bouillon · 4 strips of leek · 3 chicken bouillon cubes · 1 dessert spoon (2 tsp) vodka · 4 dessert spoons (2¾ Tbsp) olive oil · 15 cl (⅔ cup) very cold table cream · salt · freshly ground pepper

Remove the skin from the sausage and cut it into pieces. Dissolve the bouillon cubes in 80 cl (3½ cups) of boiling water and add the sausage. Whip the cream, add the vodka and 1 pinch of salt, and continue whipping until firm. Place the whipped cream in the refrigerator.

Peel the lobster, slice it into sections, and warm by slowly steaming. Meanwhile, wash, pat dry, and cook the leek strips for a few minutes in a frying pan with the olive oil.

Mix the bouillon and sausage in an electric blender (or with a hand blender) and adjust the seasoning. Divide the soup into warm soup bowls. Top with a piece of lobster, a strip of leek, and a spoonful of cream. Sprinkle with a little pepper and serve immediately.

SUGGESTED WINE PAIRING: a brut champagne

CVF RECOMMENDATION: for this recipe you can use fresh Canadian lobster, or frozen lobster.

creamy lobster bisque

A LITTLE EXPENSIVE BUT EASY - PREPARATION: 10 MIN - COOKING TIME: 15 MIN

SERVES 4

65 cl (2¾ cups) lobster bisque • 2 small frozen lobsters • 20 g (¾ oz) butter • 10 cl (½ cup) heavy sour cream • salt • freshly ground pepper • sprigs of chervil

Warm the lobster bisque over a low heat. Shell the thawed lobsters, keeping their claws whole. Halve the tails lengthwise. Cook them in a frying pan with the butter, salt, and pepper for 2 minutes. When the bisque is hot, add the cream, adjust the seasoning if necessary, and cook over a low heat for another 5 minutes.

Pour the bisque into the bowls. Add half a tail and a lobster claw to each. Garnish with the chervil and serve immediately.

SUGGESTED WINE PAIRING: a dry jurançon

pumpkin soup with foie gras ice cream

EASY AND AFFORDABLE · PREPARATION: 30 MIN · CHILLING TIME: 4H
COOKING TIME: 20 MIN

SERVES 4

1.5 kg (3 lb) pumpkin · 1 large potato · 15 cl (⅔ cup) table cream · 1 small
bunch of chives · salt · freshly ground pepper

For the ice cream: 80 g (2¾ oz) foie gras (jar or block) · 2 egg yolks · 30 cl
(1¼ cups) whole milk · 15 g (½ oz) sugar

Prepare the ice cream: heat the milk. Whisk the sugar with the egg yolks in a large bowl,
then add the hot milk while continuously whisking. Return the mixture to the saucepan,
add tiny slices of foie gras, and stir until the foie gras has melted. As soon as the mixture
is a little thick, mix and place it in the freezer for at least 4 hours (in an ice cream maker,
preferably).

Peel and chop the pumpkin and potato. Place in a casserole dish with salt and pepper and
cover with water. Simmer for 20 minutes and skim at the beginning of the cooking process.
When the vegetables are cooked, add the cream and mix until smooth.

Just before serving, warm the soup and pour it into individual soup bowls. Top with
2 small scoops of foie gras ice cream, sprinkle with the chopped chives, and serve.

SUGGESTED WINE PAIRING: a pouilly-fuissé

cauliflower

One of the quintessential winter vegetables is the cauliflower. This vegetable belongs to the cruciferous family and is native to the Middle East. There are over twenty species of cauliflower and they are harvested at different times of the year. Consequently, there are spring, summer, fall, and winter varieties. Cauliflower is almost always cooked, yet, they are most nutritious when eaten raw.

nutritional benefits

Rich in water, cauliflower is low in calories, and contains only 26 calories per 100 g (3½ oz). It is also rich in vitamin C and contains bioactive compounds, which contribute to the prevention of certain types of cancer. Cauliflower is an excellent source of B5, B6, B9, and K vitamins, and when the latter is frozen, it is full of manganese. Very high in fiber, it is a satiating vegetable and an effective bowel stimulator.

choosing and using

It is important to know how to choose a cauliflower. The head should be firm and the florets tightly closed. It can be stored for two or three days in the crisper compartment but it needs to be washed beforehand. You can choose to store only the florets or the whole cauliflower. The florets can be blanched in unsalted water and kept in the freezer for six months.

Eat the florets raw as an appetizer by dipping them in soft, white herb cheese. They can also be served as a salad with olives, tomatoes, beets, and a mustard-based vinaigrette.

Cauliflower is tasty in a gratin with a creamy white sauce, but it can also be mashed and blanched, then sautéed in a frying pan with a little butter. Try dipping the florets in batter and frying them for a few minutes in hot oil – they are delicious!

cream of cauliflower soup with scallops

EXPENSIVE BUT EASY · PREPARATION: 20 MIN · COOKING TIME: 25 MIN

SERVES 6

1 large cauliflower · 12 scallops · ½ dessert spoons (1 Tbsp) caviar · 30 g
(1 oz) butter · 35 cl (1½ cups) table cream · 1 chicken bouillon cube · salt ·
freshly ground pepper

Prepare the bouillon by diluting the cube in 50 cl (2 cups) of simmering water. Detach the
cauliflower florets and place them in 1.5 L (6 cups) of boiling salted water. When the water
comes to a boil again, cook for 20 minutes.

Meanwhile, rinse, pat dry, and halve the scallops. Using an electric blender (or hand
blender), purée the drained florets with the cream and bouillon until the mixture is smooth
and foamy. Season with salt and pepper and keep warm.

Heat the butter in a nonstick frying pan and seal the scallops for 10 seconds on each side
over a high heat. Divide the cauliflower cream soup into warm bowls, top with the scallops,
garnish with a little caviar, and serve immediately.

SUGGESTED WINE PAIRING: a condrieu

CVF RECOMMENDATION: if your budget allows, choose Sevruga, Osetra, Russian or
Aquitaine caviar. Otherwise, you can use pressed caviar (a more salty mixture of second
grade Sevruga and Beluga caviar). It is much cheaper, but very popular for its flavor.

creamy hare soup

A LITTLE TRICKY BUT REASONABLE - PREPARATION: 50 MIN - COOKING TIME: 2 H

SERVES 6

1 hare cut into pieces • 1 onion • 2 carrots • 1 celery stalk • 2 garlic cloves •
1 bunch of mixed herbs • 15 cl (⅔ cup) wine vinegar • 5 dessert spoons
(¼ cup) veal bouillon powder • 4 dessert spoons (2¾ Tbsp) duck fat • 25 cl
(1 cup) table cream + 15 cl (⅔ cup) very cold table cream • 2 slices of
farmhouse bread • 2 thin slices of Bayonne ham • 4 sprigs of chervil or flat-
leaf parsley • salt • freshly ground pepper

Set aside the saddle of hare. Peel and thinly slice the onion, carrots, celery, and garlic. Heat a little duck fat in a casserole dish and sauté the pieces of hare (excluding the saddle) with the sliced vegetables.

Add the vinegar and stir until it has evaporated. Season with salt and pepper, sprinkle with the veal bouillon powder, and add 2 L (8 cups) of boiling water. Add the mixed herbs, stir, cover, and cook for 1½ hours until the liquid reduces by a quarter.

Drain the hare and remove the bones by shredding the meat. Place the meat back in the casserole dish, remove the bunch of mixed herbs, add 25 cl (1 cup) of cream, mix thoroughly, and keep warm.

Whisk the very cold cream until it is firm and place in the refrigerator. Spread the duck fat over the slices of bread and brown in the oven.

Cut the ham into thin strips and sauté in a frying pan with a little duck fat. Using a sharp knife, cut the toast into small strips, place a slice of ham on each, and set aside.

Cook the saddle in the frying pan with the remaining fat, making sure it remains pink (about 10 minutes). Season with salt and pepper and cut evenly into round slices.

Pour the piping hot soup into bowls. Place a dessert spoon of whipped cream on top and add the bread and ham strips and the slices of saddle. Garnish with the sprigs of chervil or parsley and serve immediately.

SUGGESTED WINE PAIRING: a pernand-vergelesses

cream of chestnut and foie gras soup

A LITTLE EXPENSIVE BUT EASY · PREPARATION : 20 MIN · COOKING TIME : 30 MIN

SERVES 6

1 lobe of uncooked foie gras (about 400 g / 14 oz) · 600 g (1¼ lb) chestnuts
in water · 25 g (⅞ oz) truffle (optional) · 1 L (4 cups) milk · 4 dessert spoons
(2¾ Tbsp) chicken bouillon powder · 20 cl (¾ cup) table cream · salt · freshly
ground pepper

Dilute the chicken bouillon powder in 50 cl (2 cups) of boiling water. Boil the milk, add the
drained chestnuts, and cook for 15 minutes. Mix well to obtain a purée. Pour the purée
into a saucepan over a low heat and add the chicken bouillon (set aside 10 cl / ½ cup) and
stir thoroughly.

Devein the foie gras. Cut off a slice of 50 g (1¾ oz), mix, add the remaining chicken
bouillon, and mix again. Stir this mixture into the soup, add the cream, season with salt and
pepper, and cook for 15 minutes over a low heat.

Cut the rest of the foie gras into small slices and brown each side for 1 minute in a nonstick
pan over a high heat.

Pour the soup into warm bowls, top with the slices of foie gras, garnish evenly with the
sliced truffle and serve immediately.

SUGGESTED WINE PAIRING : a puligny-montrachet

cream of Jerusalem artichoke and foie gras soup

QUITE EXPENSIVE AND TRICKY - PREPARATION: 30 MIN - COOKING TIME: 40 MIN

SERVES 4

800 g (1¾ lb) Jerusalem artichokes • 100 g (3½ oz) butter • 10 cl (½ cup) heavy cream • 3 chicken bouillon cubes • 350 g (12¼ oz) fresh foie gras • 250 g (½ lb) puff pastry • 100 g (3½ oz) smoked streaky bacon • 1 egg yolk • salt • freshly ground pepper

Dilute the bouillon cubes in 70 cl (3 cups) of boiling water and set aside. Peel the Jerusalem artichokes and cut into round slices. Place them in a saucepan with 50 g (1¾ oz) of butter and 8 dessert spoons (5 Tbsp) of warm water. Season with salt and pepper, cover, and steam for 8 minutes.

Meanwhile, cut the foie gras into 8 small pieces about 1 cm (½ inch) thick and place in the refrigerator. Cut the bacon into small pieces (lardons). Roll out the dough and cut it into 4 circles measuring 12 cm (5 inches) in diameter. Place the bacon and dough circles in the refrigerator. In a bowl, mix the egg yolk with 1 dessert spoon (2 tsp) of water (to be used later on the pastry).

Purée the Jerusalem artichokes then pour into a saucepan. Add the heavy cream and warmed chicken bouillon and whisk. Bring to a boil and cook for 10 minutes. Remove from heat and stir in 50 g (1¾ oz) of butter. Set aside.

In a nonstick frying pan, sear the slices of foie gras until brown on both sides. Once they are crispy, remove them one by one from the pan and place them in 4 miniature casserole dishes. Fry the bacon in the foie gras cooking fat and divide equally into the 4 small serving dishes.

Preheat the oven to 210°C (410°F). Fifteen minutes before serving, fill three-quarters of the miniature casserole dishes with the cool artichoke cream. Brush a little egg yolk onto the rim of the dishes, then place the dough circles on top.

Squeeze the edges so that the dough sticks to the dish. Brush the beaten egg yolk over the entire surface of the lids. Bake for 12 minutes. Serve straight from the oven.

SUGGESTED WINE PAIRING: a chassagne-monrachet

cream of chestnut and pheasant soup

EASY AND REASONABLE - PREPARATION : 45 MIN - COOKING TIME : 1 H 20 - RESTING TIME : 12 H

SERVES 6

1 pheasant • 1 carrot • 1 onion • 1 leek • 200 g (7 oz) chestnuts in water •
1 bunch of mixed herbs • 150 g (5 oz) heavy cream • 4 dessert spoons
(2¾ Tbsp) peanut oil, divided • 1 bunch of chervil • salt • freshly ground pepper

The day before, peel and thinly slice the carrot, onion, and leek. Bone the pheasant entirely and place the legs and fillets in the refrigerator. Crush the carcass and brown in a casserole dish with 2 dessert spoons (1¼ Tbsp) of peanut oil.

Add the sliced vegetables and mixed herbs. Add 1.5 L (6 cups) of water and simmer for 1 hour. Remove from heat, leave to cool, then strain. Place the bouillon in the refrigerator overnight.

Skim the bouillon, reduce it by a third over a high heat, then add the pheasant fillets and cook for 20 minutes. Meanwhile, sauté the legs in a frying pan with the remaining oil, cover, and simmer for 20 minutes.

Remove the fillets from the bouillon and keep warm. Mix the bouillon with the cream and chestnuts (save a few for garnish) and check the seasoning.

Before serving, slice the fillets and cut the meat from the legs into small cubes. Pour the boiling hot soup into bowls, add the sliced and diced pheasant meat, garnish with the chestnuts and sprinkle with the chervil.

SUGGESTED WINE PAIRING : a red vin de pays

traditional
soups

potatoes

This tuberous vegetable, native to the Andes, can be cooked and served in various ways: baked, mashed, in salads . . . not to mention it is high in fiber and an excellent source of vitamins and minerals. Try blue or purple potatoes, they are rich in antioxidants!

nutritional benefits

Potatoes contain much more starch than most vegetables. They have an impressive amount of vitamins (such as vitamin B and C), minerals, and other compounds with health benefits, such as copper. The potato is also very rich in fiber and antioxidants.

Health tip: colorful potatoes are more beneficial to our health. This is because the antioxidant capacity in red and purple potatoes is comparable to that of cabbage or Brussel sprouts. Their nutritional value is not very high, with about 85 calories per 100 g (3½ oz) when cooked in water, so it is preferable to steam or boil potatoes.

choosing and using

The "firm" potato (or boiling potato) is low in starch and ideal for cooking. It can be used in salads, boiled, steamed, oven baked (jacket potatoes), or sautéed. Potatoes that are a little starchy do not disintegrate when cooked and can be fried, oven baked, boiled, or used in gratins and soups.

Mashed, potatoes can be spread over minced meat or flaked fish and served as a cottage or fish potato pie, which is always very popular. Diced and boiled potatoes can be mixed with mayonnaise, finely chopped celery and shallots, and served as a delicious potato salad for a summer buffet lunch

For optimal storage, keep potatoes in a dark, cool, dry environment. Avoid the refrigerator and cold temperatures that convert the starch into sugar, making potatoes sweet and gritty.

Savoyard soup

EASY AND ECONOMICAL - PREPARATION: 15 MIN - COOKING TIME: 1 H 30

SERVES 6

2 leeks • 1 turnip • 1 celery stalk • 500 g (1 lb) potatoes • 50 cl (2 cups) milk • 50 g (1¾ oz) butter • salt • freshly ground pepper • 12 slices of bread • 150 g (5 oz) Swiss cheese

Peel and wash the vegetables. Cut the leeks, turnip, and celery into thin, round slices. Melt the butter in a casserole dish and add the sliced vegetables. Sauté over a high heat for a few minutes. Cover and cook over a low heat for 20 minutes.

Cut the potatoes into small cubes and add to the vegetables with 2 L (8 cups) of warm water. Season with salt and pepper and cover. Cook for 1 hour over a low heat and stir from time to time. When 15 minutes remain, add the milk and stir.

Cut the cheese into thin strips. Toast the slices of bread, place them in a tureen, and cover the toast with the strips of cheese. Add the piping hot soup and serve.

SUGGESTED WINE PAIRING: a savoy mondeuse

CVF RECOMMENDATION: for an even more typical Savoyard soup, replace the Swiss cheese with Reblochon cheese (mild).

creamy vegetable soup

EASY AND ECONOMICAL - PREPARATION: 20 MIN - COOKING TIME: 25 MIN

SERVES 6

3 carrots • 2 turnips • 1 small celery heart • 3 bintje potatoes • 2 onions •
2 leeks • 3 garlic cloves • 1 bay leaf • 2 sprigs of thyme • 2 chicken bouillon
cubes • 10 cl (½ cup) heavy cream • 1 dessert spoon (2 tsp) olive oil • salt •
freshly ground pepper

Peel all the vegetables. Dice the carrots, turnips, and potatoes. Thinly slice the leeks, celery, onions, and garlic. Prepare a bouillon with the bouillon cubes and 1.2 L (5 cups) of boiling water.

Heat the oil in a stewpot and slowly sauté the onions and garlic. As soon as they begin to brown, add the bouillon, potatoes, carrots, leeks, celery, thyme, and bay leaf. Season with salt and pepper and simmer for 20 minutes.

When the time is up, remove the thyme and bay leaf and purée the soup (preferably with a hand or electric blender).

Pour the soup back into the stewpot and heat for 2 to 3 minutes. Add the cream and stir. Transfer the soup to a tureen and serve piping hot.

SUGGESTED WINE PAIRING: a white saint-joseph

bourriquette soup

EASY AND ECONOMICAL · PREPARATION: 15 MIN · COOKING TIME: 45 MIN

SERVES 6

3 bunches of sorrel · 4 large potatoes · 6 very fresh eggs · 2 shallots ·
2 chicken bouillon cubes · 1 dessert spoon (2 tsp) flour · 80 g (2¾ oz) butter,
divided · 8 cl (⅓ cup) white vinegar · 3 slices of stale farmhouse bread ·
2 sprigs of chervil · salt · freshly ground pepper

Thinly slice the shallots and cut the sorrel into strips. Peel the potatoes and cut them into medium-sized cubes. Melt 40 g (1½ oz) of butter in a stewpot; add the shallots, sorrel, flour, and stir. Pour 1.5 L (6 cups) of water with the bouillon cubes into the pot. Add the potatoes, season with salt and pepper, stir, and simmer for 40 minutes.

Boil 2 L (8 cups) of water with the vinegar in a large pan. Break the eggs one by one into a cup and place them carefully into the simmering water (no more than three at once). Poach for 3 minutes and remove from the pan.

Brown the diced bread in the remaining butter. Serve the bourriquette in soup bowls with the croutons, chervil, and a poached egg in the center of each bowl.

SUGGESTED WINE PAIRING: a white saint-pourçain

potato soup with toasted breadcrumbs

EASY AND ECONOMICAL - PREPARATION: 25 MIN - COOKING TIME: 25 MIN

SERVES 4

4 bintje potatoes • 2 slices of farmhouse bread • 4 very thin slices of smoked bacon • 4 dessert spoons (2¾ Tbsp) chicken bouillon powder • 1 bunch of flat-leaf parsley, divided • 2 dessert spoons (1¼ Tbsp) heavy cream • salt • freshly ground pepper

Peel, wash, and cut the potatoes into cubes. In a saucepan, boil 1 L (4 cups) of water with the chicken bouillon cubes. Simmer for 5 minutes, then add the potatoes. Cook for 20 minutes from the moment when the water starts boiling again.

Meanwhile, toast the bread until it is brown. Let it cool and then crush it into a coarse powder. Rinse the parsley and remove the leaves.

When the potatoes are cooked, add the cream, parsley (set some aside for garnish), and half of the toast. Season with salt and pepper. Blend until the mixture is smooth and creamy and keep warm.

Dry roast both sides of the bacon slices in a hot frying pan. When they are crisp, remove and drain on a paper towel. Divide the soup equally into bowls or glasses, sprinkle with the remaining toast and parsley, garnish with the crispy bacon, and serve immediately.

SUGGESTED WINE PAIRING: a white mâcon

creamy pea soup with crispy bacon

EASY AND ECONOMICAL - PREPARATION: 15 MIN - COOKING TIME: 20 MIN

SERVES 4

1 kg (2¼ lb) fresh peas • 2 white onions • 2 ordinary potatoes • 20 g (¾ oz) butter • 1 dessert spoon (2 tsp) sugar • 10 basil leaves • 10 cl (½ cup) table cream • 8 thin slices of smoked streaky bacon • 1 dessert spoon (2 tsp) oil • salt • mixed pepper

Shell the peas. Peel and thinly slice the potatoes and onions.

Melt the butter in a casserole dish. Sauté the vegetables, then add the sugar, basil, and 1 L (4 cups) of water. Season with salt, cover, and simmer for 15 minutes. When the time is up, mix the vegetables at a high speed while adding the cream.

Brown the bacon slices in an oiled frying pan until they are crisp.

Divide the soup into bowls, place the slices of bacon in the center, add a dash of pepper, and serve immediately.

SUGGESTED WINE PAIRING: a white côtes de provence

chicken consommé

EASY AND ECONOMICAL - PREPARATION: 10 MIN - COOKING TIME: 1 H 40

SERVES 4

8 chicken wings • 1 leek • 1 carrot • 1 celery stalk • 1 onion • 2 garlic cloves •
3 sprigs of parsley • 1 unwaxed orange zest • 2 cloves • 1 bay leaf •
1 dessert spoon (2 tsp) tomato purée • 2 dessert spoons (1¼ Tbsp) oil •
salt • peppercorns

Heat the oil in a stewpot and brown the chicken wings. Wash, peel, and cut the
vegetables into pieces. Add them to the pot. When all the ingredients are slightly brown,
add the tomato purée, peeled garlic, parsley sprigs, orange zest, cloves, bay leaf, and 10
peppercorns. Add salt and 2 L (8 cups) of water, stir, and leave to simmer for 1½ hours.

Allow the bouillon to stand and cool down. Strain through a fine mesh sieve and set aside.
Before serving, heat the soup until it is piping hot and serve in soup bowls as a starter, or
transform it into a sauce that can be served with poultry.

SUGGESTED WINE PAIRING: a côtes du lubéron rosé

oxtail consommé

EASY AND ECONOMICAL - PREPARATION: 20 MIN - COOKING TIME: 55 MIN

SERVES 4

1 kg (2¼ lb) oxtail sliced into short sections • 400 g (14 oz) ravioli (fresh or frozen) • 4 slices of toasted farmhouse bread • 1 leek • 1 carrot • 1 turnip • 1 celery stalk • 1 clove-studded onion • 1 garlic clove • 1 bunch of mixed herbs • 15 cl (⅔ cup) Madeira wine • salt • freshly ground pepper

Place the oxtail pieces in a pressure cooker, cover them with cold water, bring to a boil over a high heat without the lid, and boil for 5 minutes. Drain the meat and rinse the pressure cooker. Return the meat to the pot, add 1.5 L (6 cups) of cold water, and bring to a boil again.

Meanwhile, peel the vegetables and dice the celery, turnip, leek, and carrot. When the water starts boiling, add the vegetables, mixed herbs, crushed garlic, and studded onion. Close the pressure cooker, cook over a high heat, and, as soon as the valve starts hissing, reduce the heat and cook for 55 minutes.

Turn off the heat, allow the pressure to drop, then drain the meat. Shred the meat with a fork, then return it to the bouillon. Bring it to a boil, add the ravioli, and simmer for 5 minutes. Remove from the heat and add the Madeira wine, salt, and pepper and mix. Divide the consommé into warm soup bowls and serve immediately with toasted slices of farmhouse bread.

SUGGESTED WINE PAIRING: a red corbières

CVF RECOMMENDATION: if you do not have a pressure cooker, the oxtail needs to be cooked for about 2½ hours.

Jerusalem artichoke cappuccino with smoked duck breast

EASY AND ECONOMICAL - PREPARATION: 20 MIN - COOKING TIME: 30 MIN

SERVES 4

750 g (1½ lb) Jerusalem artichokes • 200 g (7 oz) potatoes • 150 g (5 oz) smoked duck breast • 2 vegetable bouillon cubes • 100 g (3½ oz) butter • 20 cl (¾ cup) table cream • 6 sprigs of parsley or chervil • salt • freshly ground pepper

Precook the un-peeled artichokes for 15 minutes in boiling water. Drain, allow to cool, and peel. Cook them for another 10 minutes in boiling salted water. Meanwhile, peel the potatoes and cook in boiling salted water for 20 minutes.

Slice the duck breast into thin strips and set aside. Dilute the bouillon cubes in 50 cl (2 cups) of very hot water. Drain the potatoes and Jerusalem artichokes and purée in a food mill. Mix the purée with the bouillon.

Place a ladle of the purée in the bowl of a food processor or a blender. Add the cream and pepper and mix until frothy. Heat the rest of the purée and butter in a saucepan over a low heat. Season with salt and pepper. Stir and remove from the heat.

Divide the purée into 4 bowls, top with the frothy creamy mixture, sprinkle with parsley or chervil, garnish with the sliced duck breast, and serve.

SUGGESTED WINE PAIRING: a red bergerac

smooth garlic soup with quail eggs

EASY AND ECONOMICAL · PREPARATION: 25 MIN · COOKING TIME: 25 MIN

SERVES 4

3 onions · 4 garlic cloves, divided · 4 quail eggs · 1 dessert spoon (2 tsp) salmon roe · 10 cl (½ cup) dry white wine · 1 dessert spoon (2 tsp) oil · 30 g (1 oz) butter, divided · ½ baguette · 1 egg yolk · 2 sprigs of thyme · ½ bay leaf · 1 dessert spoon (2 tsp) sherry vinegar · 4 sprigs of chervil · salt · freshly ground pepper

Heat the oil in a frying pan. Peel the onions and cut into strips. Place them in the pan with 3 peeled garlic cloves and brown (without burning) while stirring. Add the white wine and flambé immediately. Add 1 L (4 cups) of water, the thyme, ½ bay leaf, salt, and pepper. Cook for 20 minutes.

Meanwhile, cut out 4 small round slices from the baguette and rub with the remaining garlic clove. Fry over a low heat in 20 g (¾ oz) of butter. Set aside. Crack open the quail eggs and cook for 30 seconds in the remaining butter. Place a cooked egg on each slice of bread.

Strain the garlic soup and squeeze the ingredients to extract all the flavors. Blend the egg yolk with the vinegar and a little hot soup and pour it back into the soup. Warm the soup without letting it boil. Place the fried bread slices in warm soup bowls. Divide the soup into the bowls and garnish with the salmon roe and chervil sprigs. Add a pinch of pepper and serve.

SUGGESTED WINE PAIRING: a white côtes de provence

French onion soup

EASY AND ECONOMICAL - PREPARATION: 20 MIN - COOKING TIME: 30 MIN

SERVES 4

500 g (1 lb) onions • ½ baguette • 2 chicken bouillon cubes • 60 g (2 oz) butter • 1 dessert spoon (2 tsp) flour • 60 g (2 oz) grated comté cheese • freshly ground pepper • salt

Peel the onions and cut them into slices 0.5 cm (¼ inch) thick. Melt the butter in a casserole dish, add the onions, stir, and cook for 15 minutes over a medium heat, turning occasionally. Season with salt, add the flour, stir briskly, and cook for another 5 minutes.

Prepare the broth by diluting the bouillon cubes in 80 cl (3½ cups) of hot water. Pour over the onions in the casserole dish and simmer for 10 minutes.

Cut the bread into slices and toast. Pour the hot soup into bowls, top with the slices of toast, and sprinkle with the grated cheese. Grill for a few seconds in the oven, season with pepper, and serve.

SUGGESTED WINE PAIRING: a white sancerre

CVF RECOMMENDATION: you can also sprinkle the toast with cheese and place it in the bowls first. Add pepper and pour the hot soup over the top. You can also replace the baguette with half a loaf of farmhouse bread.

cream of onion soup with blue cheese

EASY AND ECONOMICAL - PREPARATION: 15 MIN - COOKING TIME: 30 MIN

SERVES 4

1 kg (2¼ lb) thinly sliced frozen onions • 100 g (3½ oz) bleu d'Auvergne cheese • 4 thin slices of farmhouse bread • 2 chicken bouillon cubes • 30 g (1 oz) butter • 2 dessert spoons (1¼ Tbsp) heavy cream • 4 sprigs of flat-leaf parsley • salt • freshly ground pepper

Bring 80 cl (3½ cups) of water to a boil. In a frying pan, melt the butter and sauté the onions until transparent. Crumble the bouillon cubes in the frying pan. Add the boiling water, salt, and pepper. Cover and simmer for 15 minutes.

Toast the slices of bread until golden brown and spread with the blue cheese. Add the toast to the pan and cook for 5 minutes.

Add the cream and blend the ingredients in the pan until smooth and creamy (the toast helps bind and thicken the soup). Check the seasoning, sprinkle with the parsley sprigs, and serve immediately.

SUGGESTED WINE PAIRING: a white châteauneuf du pape

CVF RECOMMENDATION: you can spread some blue cheese over thin slices of toasted bread to garnish the dish or you can fry some croutons in butter that you can serve with the soup. You can use any type of blue-veined cheese for this recipe, as long as it is not too strong.

celeriac soup with Munster cheese

EASY AND ECONOMICAL · PREPARATION: 20 MIN · COOKING TIME: 45 MIN

SERVES 4

1 small, mild Munster cheese · 1 small celeriac bulb · 1 leek · 1 large potato ·
100 g (3½ oz) diced smoked bacon (lardons) · 1 chicken bouillon cube ·
1 dessert spoon (2 tsp) cumin seeds · 4 sprigs of parsley · 20 g (¾ oz) butter ·
salt · freshly ground pepper

Peel and cut the celery and potato into cubes. Slice the leek into 4 parts without removing
the green, and wash thoroughly before thinly slicing. Bring 1.2 L (5 cups) of water to a boil
in a saucepan.

Melt the butter in a casserole dish and gently sauté the leek and bacon for about 10 minutes.
Add the crumbled bouillon cube, the diced potato, and celery. Pour the boiling water over the
top, season with pepper, add salt (but very little, because of the bacon and cheese), stir, and
leave to simmer for 35 minutes.

Meanwhile, scrape off some of the rind of the Munster and cut the cheese into small
cubes. Mix the soup (or use a food mill) until it is smooth and creamy and check
the seasoning.

Pour the soup immediately into warm bowls and sprinkle with the diced Munster, cumin
seeds, and chopped parsley.

SUGGESTED WINE PAIRING: a sylvaner

Pulses

Pulses are the dried seeds of legumes. Lentils, beans, chickpeas, and fava beans are the most common. In France, their consumption decreased during the twentieth century, but they have now become popular once again thanks to their numerous nutritional properties and the fact that they are no longer considered plain, boring food, or food for the poor. They also have other advantages – they keep longer and are very inexpensive. Our liking for regional dishes and international cuisine has also helped renew their popularity. They are, indeed, essential ingredients in cassoulet, couscous, hummus, falafel, chili con carne, and dal stew.

nutritional benefits

Pulses are rich in protein. Together with whole grains that provide essential amino acids, they form an interesting and virtuous food combination that can replace meat and eggs, with the advantage of being cholesterol-free. They do provide carbohydrates, but given their low glycemic index, digestion is slower. Their high fiber content helps prevent certain cancers and makes them satiating foods. They are also rich in mineral salts such as magnesium, calcium, iron, and group B vitamins. They contain small amounts of lipids, which are rich in essential fatty acids.

Lentils are easily digestible. They are rich in iron and calcium and also supply vitamin A. Chickpeas are recognized for their high level of fat, starch, and sodium content. Beans re rich in fiber, minerals, and vitamin B9.

choosing and using

Some pulses are known to cause bloating. This inconvenience can be avoided by following the soaking instructions on the packaging, cooking them first in fresh water, respecting the cooking time, and by adding herbs and spices that aid digestion, such as rosemary, sage, chervil, savory, ginger, and cumin. Always start cooking with cold water, and add salt only at the end.

Canned, pulses are very practical, but make sure that they are additive-free and without too much salt.

They can be used as an appetizer, starter, and as part of the main dish in vegetable tortillas, vegetable fritters, hot or cold purées, fillings, gratins, and stews. They can also be served with fresh vegetables and cereals. Some are even used in the form of flour (chickpeas, lentils), and the sprouts of some can be served in salads (lentils).

They make a great comfort food for long winter evenings. Try using them in soups, like the creamy Saint-Germain soup made from split peas.

creamy chickpea soup with smoked duck breast

EASY AND REASONABLE - PREPARATION: 15 MIN - COOKING TIME: 15 MIN

SERVES 6

1 can of plain chickpeas in water • 100 g (3½ oz) sliced smoked duck breast (vacuum packed) • 2 chicken bouillon cubes • 2 dessert spoons (1¼ Tbsp) heavy cream • 4 sprigs of chervil • 1 pinch of paprika • salt • freshly ground pepper

Prepare the bouillon by diluting the crumbled cubes in 75 cl (3¼ cups) of very hot water.

Drain the chickpeas and mix with a little bouillon to obtain 1.5 L (6 cups) of soup. Pour the soup into a saucepan and heat. Season with salt and pepper. Add the cream and paprika and slowly stir.

Remove some of the fat from the slices of duck breast. Pour the piping hot soup into bowls, top with the duck breast, sprinkle with chervil, and serve immediately.

SUGGESTED WINE PAIRING: a white arbois

CVF RECOMMENDATION: if you use dried chickpeas, soak them for 2 hours in cold water before cooking. Replace the soaking water with fresh water and simmer for 2½ to 3 hours.

international
soups

spices

Cinnamon, anise, turmeric, cardamom, saffron . . . just hearing or reading their names transports us elsewhere! Although spices are mainly used for their flavors and colors, they are also recognized for their therapeutic qualities. They can transform a vegetable and they are an essential ingredient for many international dishes – we simply cannot do without them!

nutritional benefits

There are very few spices without a therapeutic benefit. Some are deemed to be natural antiseptics and some, like anise (or star anise), turmeric, and cardamom, assist the digestive process. Star anise is also considered an antispasmodic. Cardamom helps combat abdominal bloating and respiratory diseases. Turmeric contains antioxidant and anti-inflammatory properties. Another advantage of spices is that they contain no calories.

choosing and using

More often than not, spices come in the shape of seeds, berries, bark, powder, sticks (cinnamon), or pistils (saffron). When purchasing, be demanding, because depending on their quality and freshness, their aroma can vary considerably. The key to success when using spices is finding the right amount to use. Add the spice gradually to avoid masking the flavors of the other ingredients. Too much of a spice can make the dish unappetizing.

Star anise is delicious in tea or a marinade, and it can be used with honey to add a little flavor to oven-baked pears, apples, or peaches, even mulled wine. It is also often used in gingerbread.

Turmeric can be used as a coloring agent. It goes very well with rice, potatoes, eggs, vegetables, and fish.

Cardamom is one of the most popular spices in Indian cuisine. It comes in small green and white pods, which contain black seeds. It is best to buy cardamom in pods and to open the pod at the last minute. It is used in curries, marinades, and desserts, or in a simple cup of hot milk.

Make your soups a little more exotic by sprinkling them with a little spice! Try adding a pinch of cumin to a creamy carrot soup or some cinnamon to an orange soup . . . they will only taste better!

orient express soup

EASY AND ECONOMICAL · SOAKING TIME: 30 MIN · PREPARATION: 20 MIN
COOKING TIME: 15 MIN

SERVES 4

150 g (5 oz) rice noodles • 100 g (3½ oz) chicken breast • 8 dried black mushrooms • 200 g (7 oz) shrimp • 2 onions • 1 garlic clove • 1 fresh ginger rhizome • 1 strip of red pepper or 1 small chili pepper • 3 chicken bouillon cubes • 3 sprigs of cilantro • 1 dessert spoon (2 tsp) oil • salt • freshly ground pepper • pan-roasted sesame seeds (optional)

Soak the mushrooms for 30 minutes in hot water. Soak the noodles in a separate container for 10 minutes. Steam or microwave the chicken breasts.

Peel and chop the onions, garlic, and ginger. Cut the red pepper (or chili) into small pieces. Pour the oil into a casserole dish and gently fry the ingredients for 5 minutes.

Dilute the bouillon cubes in 80 cl (3½ cups) of very hot water. Pour the bouillon into the dish, bring to a boil, and add the chopped chicken, noodles, and drained mushrooms. Season with salt and pepper, simmer for 5 minutes, and add the shrimp and finely chopped cilantro.

Divide the soup into bowls and serve. You can garnish the soup with some pan-roasted sesame seeds.

SUGGESTED WINE PAIRING: an anjou rosé

chicken curry soup

EASY AND ECONOMICAL - PREPARATION: 30 MIN - COOKING TIME: 1 H 10

SERVES 6

1.5 kg (3 lb) free-range, pre-cut chicken • 200 g (7 oz) basmati rice • 3 onions •
4 leeks (white part only) • 2 celery stalks • 50 g (1¾ oz) butter • 40 cl
(1¾ cups) coconut milk • 3 level dessert spoons (2 Tbsp) curry powder (mild)
• 60 g (2 oz) flaked almonds • 2 dessert spoons (1¼ Tbsp) flour • 2 chicken
bouillon cubes • 1 small bunch of cilantro • 1 clove • salt • freshly ground pepper

Clean the leeks, remove the strings from the celery, and cut both into thick, round slices.
Peel and thinly slice the onions.

Melt the butter in a casserole dish. Brown the chicken pieces and drain. Fry the onion
for 5 minutes and add the celery and leeks. Cook over a low heat for 10 minutes, stirring
regularly. Sprinkle with the flour and curry powder and stir briskly. Crumble the bouillon
cubes into the dish and add 2 L (8 cups) of hot water. Stir, add the chicken and clove,
partially cover, adjust the heat, and simmer for 1 hour.

Meanwhile, dry roast the almonds in a frying pan and cook the rice in salted boiling water
for about 12 minutes. Drain and set aside.

After 1 hour, use a skimming ladle to remove the chicken from the casserole dish. Bone
the chicken, remove the skin, and shred the meat with a fork. Place the dish over a low
heat and add the rice, chicken, and coconut milk. Season with salt and pepper and leave
to simmer for 10 minutes. Serve the soup piping hot and sprinkle with the chopped cilantro
and roasted almond flakes.

SUGGESTED WINE PAIRING: a dry white bergerac

oriental soup

EASY AND ECONOMICAL · PREPARATION: 25 MIN · COOKING TIME: 40 MIN

SERVES 6

1 kg (2¼ lb) onions · 1 kg (2¼ lb) tomatoes · 1 small can of chickpeas ·
600 g (1½ lb) shelled fava beans (fresh or frozen) · 1 bouillon cube · 2 dessert
spoons (1¼ Tbsp) olive oil · ½ dessert spoon (1 tsp) harissa · 1 dessert spoon
(2 tsp) ground cumin · 1 bunch of cilantro · salt

Boil, peel, seed, and crush the tomatoes with a fork. Chop the onions. Pour the oil into
a casserole dish and sauté the onions until they are transparent.

Add the crushed tomatoes, drained chickpeas, cumin, harissa, and bouillon cube. Season
with salt and cover with 1.5 L (6 cups) of hot water. Stir, bring to a boil, and simmer for
30 minutes.

Meanwhile, cook the beans for 10 minutes in salted boiling water, drain, and cool under
cold, running water. Discard their skin and set aside.

Just before serving, add the beans to the soup and cook for 5 minutes. Sprinkle with the
chopped cilantro and serve piping hot.

SUGGESTED WINE PAIRING: a white bergerac

CVF RECOMMENDATION: pre-packed, peeled, and sliced frozen onions are very practical
for this type of recipe. They will save you time and tears.

cream of carrot and orange soup

EASY AND ECONOMICAL - PREPARATION: 15 MIN - COOKING TIME: 20 MIN

SERVES 4

500 g (1 lb) carrots • 1 chicken bouillon cube • 1 freshly squeezed orange • 10 g (⅓ oz) sugar • ½ dessert spoon (1 tsp) cumin seeds • 1 bunch of cilantro • salt • Espelette pepper

Prepare the bouillon cube in 75 cl (3¼ cups) of water, then add the peeled, washed, and sliced carrots. Add the cumin seeds, salt, and pepper, and simmer until the carrots are tender.

Wash the cilantro and remove the leaves. Thoroughly mix all the ingredients together, including the orange juice, sugar, and cilantro.

SUGGESTED WINE PAIRING: a dry anjou

Moroccan harira

EASY AND ECONOMICAL - PREPARATION : 15 MIN - COOKING TIME : 45 MIN

SERVES 4

1 small can of chickpeas • ½ bunch of cilantro • ½ bunch of flat-leaf parsley • 3 celery stalks • 1 onion • 1 large can of peeled tomatoes • 3 dessert spoons (2 Tbsp) tomato paste • 300 g (10 oz) shoulder of lamb, divided • 4 dessert spoons (2¾ Tbsp) olive oil • ½ dessert spoon (1 tsp) ground ginger • 1 small cinnamon stick • 1 pinch of turmeric • 1 dessert spoon (2 tsp) long grain rice • 80 g (2¾ oz) flour • salt • freshly ground pepper

Preheat the oven to 180°C (350°F). Drain the chickpeas, then rinse several times. Drain the tomatoes, then mix them with the tomato paste to obtain a coulis. Wash the celery, peel the onion, and coarsely chop both.

Cut 50 g (1¾ oz) of the shoulder of lamb into small cubes. Put the rest in an ovenproof dish, drizzle with 1 dessert spoon (2 tsp) of olive oil, and cook for 45 minutes.

Wash, drain, and chop the herbs. Pour the olive oil into a casserole dish and sauté the rest of the lamb, spices, and onion for 5 minutes. Add the tomato coulis, celery, and chickpeas. Season with salt and pepper and simmer for 30 minutes. Add 1 L (4 cups) of water, the herbs, and rice, and continue cooking for another 15 minutes.

Remove the cinnamon stick. Mix a ladle of broth with the flour, then add to the soup. Continue cooking for 10 minutes until the harira thickens. Check the seasoning and serve with the sliced shoulder of lamb.

SUGGESTED WINE PAIRING : a côtes de provence rosé

curried Jerusalem artichoke soup

EASY AND ECONOMICAL - PREPARATION: 10 MIN - COOKING TIME: 35 MIN

SERVES 4

500 g (1 lb) Jerusalem artichokes • 1 chicken bouillon cube • ½ dessert spoon (1 tsp) liquid honey • ½ dessert spoon (1 tsp) curry powder • 15 cl (⅔ cup) table cream • 2 dessert spoons (1¼ Tbsp) olive oil • salt • white pepper

Dilute the bouillon cube in 75 cl (3¼ cups) of boiling water. Wash the artichokes and cut them into cubes (without peeling them).

In a casserole dish, heat the olive oil and add the diced artichokes. While stirring, sauté for 5 minutes over a low heat. Add the curry, and slightly caramelize with the honey.

Pour the chicken bouillon into the casserole dish and bring to a boil. Add the cream, cover, and simmer for 30 minutes. Mix the ingredients in an electric blender (or with a hand blender) until the soup is smooth and creamy. Season with salt and pepper and serve hot.

SUGGESTED WINE PAIRING: a pouilly-vinzelles

carrot and cumin soup with hummus

EASY AND ECONOMICAL - PREPARATION: 15 MIN - COOKING TIME: 35 MIN

SERVES 4

600 g (1½ lb) carrots • 1 peeled, thinly sliced onion • ½ dessert spoon (1 tsp) ground cumin • 1 dessert spoon (2 tsp) olive oil • 1 vegetable bouillon cube • ½ dessert spoon (1 tsp) coarse gray salt

For the hummus: 250 g (½ lb) canned chickpeas • 1 peeled, chopped garlic clove • 1 dessert spoon (2 tsp) sesame oil • juice of ½ lemon • 1 dessert spoon (2 tsp) finely chopped cilantro (or flat-leaf parsley) • salt • freshly ground pepper

Wash and peel the carrots. Grate 1 carrot and set aside; cut the others into round slices. Heat the olive oil in a casserole dish and add the chopped onion. Sprinkle with the cumin, stir, and cook over a medium heat for 2 minutes.

Add the carrots, bouillon cube, and coarse gray salt. Add enough water to cover the carrots. Cover the dish and cook for 30 minutes over a low heat.

Mix all the ingredients for the hummus and set aside.

Mix the soup then pour it into individual soup bowls. Top with a spoonful of hummus and garnish with the grated carrot.

SUGGESTED WINE PAIRING: a white irouléguy

creamy mussel soup with chorizo

EASY AND ECONOMICAL - PREPARATION: 30 MIN - COOKING TIME: 20 MIN

SERVES 6

2 L (8 cups) mussels • 12 thin, quite large slices of chorizo • 30 cl (1¼ cups) heavy sour cream • 3 dessert spoons (2 Tbsp) fish bouillon powder • 250 g (½ lb) frozen julienne vegetables • 1 onion • 1 garlic clove • 2 dessert spoons (1¼ Tbsp) olive oil • 2 saffron pistils • 6 sprigs of chervil • 15 cl (⅔ cup) dry white wine • salt • freshly ground pepper

Peel and thinly slice the garlic and onion. Carefully clean the mussels. Heat the oil in a casserole dish and sauté (without browning) the julienne vegetables garlic and onion. Add the wine and mussels. Stir, cover, and cook over a medium heat until all the mussels have opened.

Drain the mussels in a colander over a saucepan to recover the cooking juices. Remove their shells and set them aside. Dilute the bouillon in the mussel juices with 1.5 L (6 cups) of water. Add the saffron and bring to a boil. Boil over a high heat for 5 minutes before adding the cream. Season with salt and pepper and blend until smooth and creamy. Keep warm over a low heat.

Remove the skin from the chorizo and cook the slices in a hot frying pan. When they begin to "curl," turn them over and, once they are crispy, remove from the pan and drain on a paper towel. Pour the creamy soup into bowls and add the deshelled mussels. Top with the crispy chorizo slices and garnish with the sprigs of chervil. Serve immediately.

SUGGESTED WINE PAIRING: a pinot blanc

aromatic plants

Just a few grams of one of these naturally scented and flavored plants are sufficient to transform the taste and color of a simple dressing. We can use their leaves or, in certain cases, their rhizomes (roots). They offer us an incredible range of flavors and colors.

nutritional benefits

Although these plants are only eaten in small quantities, they do, nevertheless, enrich our diets with antioxidants and minerals such as iron, potassium, and calcium. By adding flavor to our dishes, they help us reduce our consumption of salt and fat. To make the most of their nutritional benefits, it is recommended to eat them fresh, or frozen.

Chervil is rich in vitamins C, E, B2, K, and B9, as well as provitamin A. It also provides calcium and manganese.

Lemongrass, which has an aroma similar to that of lemon verbena, helps digestion and is refreshing.

Cilantro provides vitamin E, potassium, copper, and manganese. It is also rich in vitamins K, C, and B9.

Ginger has antioxidant properties and it stimulates digestion. It is rich in carbohydrates and vitamin C.

Parsley has a high vitamin C content and is a source of provitamin A and vitamins B9 and E. It is rich in potassium, calcium, and iron. It also has diuretic properties and is a natural antispasmodic.

choosing and using

Aromatic plants are available fresh, dehydrated, in seeds, in powders, or frozen. For hot dishes, adding the fresh herbs in two stages increases the flavor: add half at the beginning of the cooking process and the other half at the end, just before serving. It is recommended to chop them beforehand.

More often than not we use their leaves, but they can also be used in bunches to flavor bouillons or cooking water. Parsley sprigs are perfect as a bouquet garnish. Some aromatic plants, such as verbena, are not eaten but are used to prepare herbal tea.

Fresh ginger can be grated, sliced into small sticks or squeezed. A piece of ginger measuring 1 cm (½ inch weighs about 5 g (⅙ oz) and 15 g (½ oz) of unpeeled ginger represents about 10 g (⅓ oz) of grated ginger. Add a subtle touch of originality and enhance the flavor of your soups by sprinkling them with a little ginger just before serving.

beef and lemongrass consommé

EASY AND ECONOMICAL · PREPARATION: 20 MIN · COOKING TIME: 2 H

SERVES 6

800 g (1¾ lb) oxtail cut into pieces • 1 celery stalk • 200 g (7 oz) carrots •
200 g (7 oz) turnips • 250 g (½ lb) zucchini • 100 g (3½ oz) rice noodles •
2 lemongrass bulbs • 1 bunch of cilantro • 1 onion • 2 cloves • ¼ dessert spoon
(½ tsp) peppercorns • ¼ dessert spoon (½ tsp) coarse sea salt • table salt •
freshly ground pepper

Place the oxtail pieces in a casserole dish and cover with a significant amount of cold
water. Stud the onion with cloves. Add the celery stalk, clove studded onion, peppercorns,
and sea salt. Bring to a boil and simmer for 1 hour and 45 minutes.

Meanwhile, peel and cut the carrots and turnips into round slices. Discard both ends
of the zucchini and cut into round slices. Slice the lemongrass into thin strips.

When the meat is cooked, remove it from the dish with a skimming ladle. Strain the
bouillon and pour it back into the casserole dish. Shred the meat and discard the bones.

Cook the noodles in boiling water for 3 minutes. Drain and set aside. Bring the bouillon to
a boil. Add the lemongrass and vegetables. Season with salt and pepper and simmer for
4 minutes. Add the noodles and meat and cook for another 3 minutes. Garnish with the
chopped cilantro, remove from heat, and serve.

SUGGESTED WINE PAIRING: a bordeaux rosé

chicken and lemongrass soup

EASY AND ECONOMICAL - PREPARATION: 10 MIN - COOKING TIME: 10 MIN

SERVES 4

2 celery stalks • 2 carrots • 4 sprigs of lemongrass • 1 ginger rhizome •
1 small red pepper • 2 dessert spoons (1¼ Tbsp) olive oil • zest of 1 lemon
• 8 scallions • 8 spears of baby corn • 3 chicken breasts • 2 heaped dessert
spoons (1¼ Tbsp) chopped cilantro leaves • salt • freshly ground pepper

Peel the carrots, lemongrass, and ginger. Coarsely grate the carrots. Peel the lemon
and set aside the zest.

Remove the stalk and the seeds from the pepper. Chop the celery, ginger, pepper,
and the tender hearts of the lemongrass.

Heat the oil in a wok and sauté the vegetables, lemongrass, ginger, and zest for
2 minutes. Add 1.25 L (5 cups) of boiling water and boil for 5 minutes.

Clean the onions and slice the chicken into strips. Add the onions, baby corn, and chicken
to the ingredients in the wok. Cook for 3 minutes. Season with salt and pepper. Divide the
soup into individual bowls and sprinkle with the cilantro.

SUGGESTED WINE PAIRING: a condrieu

chorba

EASY AND ECONOMICAL - PREPARATION: 30 MIN - COOKING TIME: 2H20

SERVES 6

800 g (1¾ lb) lamb pieces (neck of lamb or cutlets) • 4 small zucchini •
1 small can peeled tomatoes • 1 small can chickpeas • 2 onions • 75 g (2⅔ oz)
vermicelli • ½ bunch of cilantro • ½ bunch of mint • 1 dessert spoon (2 tsp)
olive oil • ½ dessert spoon (1 tsp) ground cumin • 2 pinches of chili • salt •
freshly ground pepper

Drain and chop the tomatoes, then peel and slice the onions. Rinse the zucchini, discard
the ends, and cut into thick round slices.

Heat the oil in a casserole dish, brown the meat on all sides, then add the onions and
zucchini slices. Stir for 2 minutes. Add the tomatoes, drained chickpeas, cumin, pepper,
and salt. Stir, cover with water, bring to a boil, reduce the heat, cover, and simmer for
2 hours over a low heat. With 10 minutes remaining, add the tied bunches of cilantro and
mint.

Drain the meat and herbs with a skimmer. Boil the bouillon over a high heat for a few
minutes until it thickens. Add the vermicelli and cook for 2 minutes. Return the meat to
the soup, stir, and serve piping hot.

SUGGESTED WINE PAIRING: a bandol rosé

cream of asparagus soup and mint pea purée

EASY AND ECONOMICAL · PREPARATION: 15 MIN · COOKING TIME: 30 MIN

SERVES 4

1 kg (2¼ lb) white asparagus · 300 g (10 oz) shelled peas (fresh or frozen) · 25 cl (1 cup) table cream · 10 fresh mint leaves, divided · salt · freshly ground pepper

Prepare the soup: wash and pat dry the asparagus. Using a vegetable peeler, peel from the top downward (keep the peelings), then cut into small pieces. Place the peelings in a casserole dish, cover with water, add a little salt, and simmer for 10 minutes.

When the time is up, strain the bouillon and discard the peels. Pour the bouillon back into the dish and add the sliced asparagus and the cream. Cook for 15 minutes over a low heat. Using an electric or hand blender, mix the ingredients. Season with salt and pepper, strain, and allow to cool before placing in the refrigerator.

Prepare the pea purée: cook the peas for 5 minutes in boiling salted water and drain. Cool them down with ice cold water, drain again, and mix with 6 mint leaves and a little bouillon water until the mixture resembles a thick purée. Season with salt and pepper.

Divide the pea purée equally into tall or short glasses. Top with the asparagus soup, garnish with the rest of the mint, and serve chilled.

SUGGESTED WINE PAIRING: a cour-cheverny

carrot soup with argan oil

EASY AND ECONOMICAL - PREPARATION AND COOKING TIME: 30 MIN

SERVES 4

600 g (1¼ lb) grated carrots • 100 g (3½ oz) chopped onions (frozen) • juice of 2 oranges • 1 chicken bouillon cube • ½ dessert spoon (1 tsp) ground cumin • 15 g (½ oz) butter • 2 dessert spoons (1¼ Tbsp) argan oil • 8 sprigs of fresh cilantro • salt • freshly ground pepper

Melt the butter in a casserole dish and cook the onions for 5 minutes. Add the carrots, cumin, and crumbled bouillon cube. Add 1 L (4 cups) of water, salt, and pepper, partially cover, and simmer for 15 minutes.

When the time is up, mix the soup (in a blender or with a hand blender) while adding the orange juice. Divide the soup into individual bowls.

Drizzle the argan oil over the soup, garnish with the cilantro sprigs, and serve immediately.

SUGGESTED WINE PAIRING: a coteaux varois rosé

creamy coral lentil and pumpkin soup

EASY AND ECONOMICAL **·** PREPARATION: 10 MIN **·** COOKING TIME: 20 MIN

SERVES 4

120 g (4¼ oz) coral lentils **·** 1 onion **·** 400 g (14 oz) pumpkin **·** 10 cl (½ cup) coconut milk **·** ½ chicken bouillon cube **·** 1 dessert spoon (2 tsp) olive oil, divided **·** 1 pinch of ground cumin **·** 4 pinches of shredded coconut **·** 2 sprigs of cilantro **·** salt **·** freshly ground pepper

Rinse the lentils and drain. Peel the pumpkin and cut it into cubes. Peel, thinly slice, and sauté the onion until soft in 1 dessert spoon (2 tsp) of oil in a frying pan. Sprinkle with the cumin.

Add the pumpkin and lentils and stir with a spatula for 3 minutes. Dilute the bouillon cube in 50 cl (2 cups) of hot water, pour into the pan, and bring to a boil. Reduce the heat, add the coconut milk, salt, and stir. Cover and cook for 15 to 20 minutes (the lentils should be tender and easy to mix).

Mix the ingredients in a blender with the remaining oil (add a little water if necessary) and season with pepper. Divide the soup equally into 4 bowls, sprinkle with the shredded coconut, garnish with the cilantro, and serve.

SUGGESTED WINE PAIRING: a chablis

Italian tomato soup

EASY AND ECONOMICAL - PREPARATION: 15 MIN - COOKING TIME: 25 MIN

SERVES 4

4 slices of stale farmhouse bread • 2 cans of peeled tomatoes • 80 g (2¾ oz) parmesan • 2 onions • 2 garlic cloves • 1 small jar of pesto • ½ dessert spoon (1 tsp) sugar • 4 dessert spoons (2¾ Tbsp) olive oil • salt • freshly ground pepper

Peel and finely chop the garlic and onions. Sauté (without browning) in the oil in a casserole dish. Drain the tomatoes and set aside the juice. Cut the tomatoes and bread into pieces and add them to the onions. Season with salt and pepper, add the sugar, and stir. Cook for 10 minutes, stirring occasionally. Add the tomato juice and cook for another 10 minutes.

Put 1 teaspoon of pesto and some grated parmesan cheese in each bowl. Add the soup and serve.

SUGGESTED WINE PAIRING: a bandol rosé

instant borscht

EASY AND ECONOMICAL - PREPARATION: 10 MIN - COOKING TIME: 30 MIN

SERVES 4

250 g (½ lb) mixed, diced vegetables (frozen) · 200 g (7 oz) shredded red cabbage (pre-packed) · 1 cooked beet · 200 g (7 oz) diced smoked bacon (lardons) · 4 dessert spoons (2¾ Tbsp) heavy cream · 1 dessert spoon (2 tsp) wine vinegar · 2 beef bouillon cubes · salt · freshly ground pepper

Heat 1.5 L (6 cups) of water with the vinegar in a saucepan. Add the crumbled bouillon cubes. Once the liquid has boiled, reduce the heat and leave to simmer. Add the bacon, cabbage, and diced vegetables. Season generously with salt and pepper and simmer for 20 minutes.

Meanwhile, peel the beet, coarsely chop, and set aside. Divide the heavy cream equally into 4 bowls.

Toward the end of the cooking process, add the chopped beet to the ingredients in the saucepan and simmer for 5 minutes. Divide the borscht into the bowls and serve immediately.

SUGGESTED WINE PAIRING: a tavel

CVF RECOMMENDATION: to make this typical Russian soup a little richer, you can add 200 g (7 oz) of cooked beef. Cut the meat into small cubes or thin strips and place in the saucepan at the same time as the beet.

instant Andalusian gazpacho

EASY AND ECONOMICAL - PREPARATION: 20 MIN - COOKING TIME: 5 MIN

SERVES 4

1 L (4 cups) plain tomato coulis • ½ red pepper • ½ green pepper •
½ cucumber • 4 small white onions • 1 garlic clove • 4 slices of white sandwich
bread, divided • 1 dessert spoon (2 tsp) balsamic vinegar • 8 dessert spoons
(5 Tbsp) olive oil, divided • salt • freshly ground pepper

Peel and finely chop the onions. Wash the peppers and cut them into tiny cubes. Peel
the cucumber and cut in half lengthwise. Remove the seeds and cut into tiny cubes. Peel
the garlic clove and halve. Before finely chopping the garlic, use it to rub the bottom of a
fondue pot or a glazed earthenware bowl.

Crumble a slice of bread into the pot or bowl. Add 4 dessert spoons (2¾ Tbsp) of oil, the
garlic, vegetables, vinegar, and tomato coulis. Add salt and pepper and mix. Place in the
refrigerator until it is time to serve.

Just before serving, remove the crust from the remaining slices of bread and cut into
triangles. Brown in a pan with the remaining oil and drain on a paper towel. Add some ice
cubes to the gazpacho, garnish with the toasted bread, and serve immediately.

SUGGESTED WINE PAIRING: a bandol rosé

CVF RECOMMENDATION: to save time, you can use 6 dessert spoons (4 Tbsp) of diced
frozen peppers (mixture of green and red) and ready-to-use croutons.

cream of shiitake mushroom soup

EASY AND ECONOMICAL - PREPARATION: 30 MIN - COOKING TIME: 40 MIN

SERVES 6

600 g (1¼ lb) shiitake mushrooms (or black forest mushrooms) • 500 g
(1 lb) potatoes • 3 medium-sized leeks • 150 g (5 oz) onions • 3 garlic cloves •
2 chicken bouillon cubes • 20 cl (¾ cup) table cream • 30 g (1 oz) butter •
1 dessert spoon (2 tsp) olive oil • a few sprigs of chervil • nutmeg • salt •
freshly ground pepper

Clean and blanch the mushrooms for 2 minutes in salted boiling water. Drain, cool under
running water, and squeeze to drain them thoroughly. Peel the potatoes, leeks, onions, and
cut all these vegetables into cubes. Peel the garlic.

Melt the butter in a stewpot and brown the diced vegetables. Add half of the mushrooms
and cook for 10 minutes over a medium heat. Dilute the bouillon cubes in 60 cl (2½ cups)
of hot water and pour into the pot. Add the garlic, season with salt, pepper, and nutmeg,
and cook for 30 minutes over a low heat.

Heat the olive oil in a frying pan and sauté the rest of the mushrooms for 2 to 3 minutes.
Add the cream to the ingredients in the stewpot and mix. Divide the soup into individual
bowls, add the sautéed mushrooms, and garnish with the chervil. Serve piping hot.

SUGGESTED WINE PAIRING: a dry white bergerac

index

credits & acknowledgements

PHOTOGRAPHS

Jérôme Bilic (p. 22, 73, 113, 124, 131, 153, 163) ; Beatriz Da Costa (p. 146) ; Christine Fleurent (p. 17, 25, 33, 104, 188) ; Jean-Blaise Hall (p. 170); Pierre Hussenot (p. 83, 133) ; David Japy (p. 166) ; Valérie Lhomme (p. 27, 49, 98, 154, 157) ; Jean-Jacques Magis (p. 13, 157) ; Jean-François Mallet (p. 41, 103) ; Alain Muriot (p. 140, 175) ; Loïc Nicoloso (p. 21, 28, 45, 53, 90, 97, 169) ; Jean-François Rivière (p. 11, 37, 119, 136); Amélie Roche (p. 174) ; Laurent Rouvrais (couverture, p. 14, 47, 67, 75, 95, 101, 143, 158, 181); Christophe Valentin (p. 78, 161) ; Philipp Vaures Santa Maria (p. 50, 60) ; Pierre-Louis Viel (p. 57, 58, 151, 176) ; DR (p. 123).

RECIPES

Bruno Ballureau, Blandine Boyer, Michele Carles, Manuella Chantepie, Christian Constant, Solveig Darrigo, Ilan Waiche, Irène Karsenty, Les Sœurs Scotto, Marie Leteuré, Valérie Lhomme, Catherine Madani, Jean-François Mallet, Pascale Mosnier, Éric Solal.

ACKNOWLEDGEMENTS

Maison Trevier : p. 84 ; Éric Frechon : p. 171 ; Karine Valentin for the wine pairings.

MARIE CLAIRE EDITION CONTRIBUTORS:
Editorial director: Irène Karsenty
Art director: Francis Seguin
Editorial assistant: Pauline Arnold
Publishing director: Thierry Lamarre
Creation: Mathilde Joannès
Iconographic research: Sylvie Creusy
Graphic design and layout: Either Studio

WHITECAP BOOKS EDITION CONTRIBUTORS:
Translation: Susan Allen Maurin
Editor: Michelle van der Merwe
Typesetting: Robert Ondzik
Proofreading: Patrick Geraghty
Cover design: Andrew Bagatella

Printed in Romania

Library and Archives Canada Cataloguing in Publication available from Library and Archives Canada

We acknowledge the financial support of the Government of Canada and the Province of British Columbia through the Book Publishing Tax Credit.
Nous reconnaissons l'appui financier du gouvernement du Canada et la province de la Colombie-Britannique par le Book Publishing Tax Credit.

21 20 19 18 17 16 15   1 2 3 4 5 6 7